AI-Powered Finance

Harnessing Artificial Intelligence to Transform Banking, Investment, and Risk Management

Written by
Eric LeBouthillier

AcraSolution | 2025 1st Edition
www.acrasolution.com

Preface

Why This Book Exists

The world of finance is entering a profound shift — driven not by regulations or tradition, but by algorithms, data, and artificial intelligence. *AI in Finance* was written for forward-thinking professionals, business leaders, startup founders, and lifelong learners who want to understand how AI is transforming the financial world — from investment strategies to fraud detection, compliance, and beyond.

This is not a book about code. It's a strategic guide written in plain, professional language for people who make decisions, build companies, and shape industries. Whether you're an experienced investor, a finance executive, or simply AI-curious, this book was designed to help you make sense of the future of finance without needing a PhD in computer science.

— *Eric LeBouthillier*
Founder, AcraSolution

For permission requests or inquiries, contact the publisher through the website : www.acrasolution.com

LEGAL DISCLAIMER

This publication is intended solely for informational and educational purposes. It does not constitute legal, financial, medical, or professional advice. The content is not a substitute for consultation with qualified experts or licensed professionals in the relevant fields.

Portions of this work have been created or assisted by artificial intelligence (AI) tools. While every reasonable effort has been made to review, fact-check, and edit the content for clarity and accuracy, AI-generated information may occasionally contain errors, omissions, or generalized statements. The author and publisher do not guarantee the accuracy, completeness, or reliability of the information provided.

Readers are strongly encouraged to seek independent advice tailored to their personal circumstances from qualified legal, financial, healthcare, or compliance professionals before making decisions or taking action based on this content.

References to specific products, services, companies, websites, or technologies do not imply endorsement or affiliation unless explicitly stated. All trademarks and brand names mentioned remain the property of their respective owners.

The author and publisher disclaim any liability, loss, or risk incurred directly or indirectly from the use or misuse of this publication. This includes, but is not limited to, damages of any kind — including incidental, special, or consequential — arising out of the reliance on the material presented.

All references to laws, regulations, security standards, or industry guidelines are intended for general awareness only and may not reflect the most current legal developments. This publication is not intended to create, and receipt does not constitute, a client relationship with the author, publisher, or any affiliated entity.

By reading, accessing, or applying the content in this publication, you agree to do so at your own risk. If you do not accept these terms, you are advised to discontinue use of this material immediately.

Who This Book Is For

This book is for:

- Financial professionals and business leaders seeking to future-proof their strategies
- Entrepreneurs and FinTech founders exploring AI opportunities
- Policy makers, educators, and researchers who want to understand AI's real-world financial impact
- Curious readers who want a clear, insightful, and non-technical explanation of AI's role in modern finance

If you've been looking for a resource that explains *what's happening*, *why it matters*, and *what to do about it* — this is for you.

What to Expect From This Book

This book offers a clear, practical, and non-technical guide to how AI is reshaping finance. Each chapter delivers real-world insights, case studies, and strategic takeaways — without fluff, hype, or unnecessary complexity.

You won't find dense academic theory or code-heavy explanations here. Instead, you'll get straightforward, professional content designed for business leaders, innovators, and decision-makers who need to understand what AI means for finance — and how to respond.

If you're looking for clarity over complexity and substance over buzzwords, you're in the right place.

Table of Contents

Chapter 1: The Financial AI Revolution

The financial industry is no stranger to technology—but AI is not just another step in digital evolution. It's a break from tradition so significant that ignoring it is no longer an option. Across banking, investment, insurance, and accounting, artificial intelligence is reshaping how money moves, how risks are calculated, and how decisions are made. For small and mid-sized firms, the stakes are rising fast: adopt, adapt—or get left behind.

AI isn't just a tool for Wall Street giants anymore. It's now in the hands of leaner firms, startups, and even solo practitioners who understand how to wield it strategically. This chapter demystifies the financial AI revolution so you can lead with clarity—not chase it with confusion.

Why Finance Is Ripe for AI Disruption

Finance runs on information. Spreadsheets, transactions, contracts, signals, statements—these are the lifeblood of the industry. AI thrives in exactly this environment: one saturated with data, patterns, and high-value decisions.

What makes finance especially vulnerable—and opportune—for disruption?

- **Data Abundance**: Years of structured data (like accounting records) and growing volumes of unstructured data (like call transcripts or social media sentiment) are now usable.
- **Process Complexity**: Many financial operations are rule-based but involve human fatigue and inconsistency—ideal for automation.
- **High Stakes and Speed**: Markets move fast. The ability to analyze, act, and adapt instantly is no longer optional.
- **Regulatory Pressure**: Compliance is increasingly costly and difficult; AI can dramatically reduce false positives and streamline audits.

SMBs face a particularly sharp curve. While they may not have enterprise-scale budgets, they are now able to deploy scalable AI tools that were previously out of reach—often at a fraction of the cost.

Core AI Technologies: ML, NLP, Computer Vision

Understanding the foundational tools of financial AI is essential. Here's a breakdown in plain terms:

- **Machine Learning (ML)**: This is about systems learning from historical data to predict or classify future events. Think fraud detection, credit scoring, or customer churn models.
- **Natural Language Processing (NLP)**: NLP allows machines to understand and analyze human language. It powers chatbots, reads legal contracts, or interprets market sentiment from news articles.
- **Computer Vision**: Less common but increasingly relevant. It's used in document verification (like scanning checks or IDs) and facial recognition in digital KYC (Know Your Customer) processes.

These aren't theoretical tools—they're deployed in live systems today, streamlining onboarding, risk scoring, investment analysis, and more.

From Traditional Models to AI-First Thinking

Traditionally, financial models were rule-based and manually constructed. AI reverses that. Instead of hand-coding decision trees, AI learns from the past to navigate the future.

This shift is profound:

- **Reactive → Predictive**: AI systems can forecast defaults, fraud attempts, or price shifts before they happen.
- **Manual → Automated**: Tasks once performed by junior analysts—like data cleaning or reconciliation—are now automated with higher accuracy.

- **Standardized → Personalized**: AI tailors financial advice, lending terms, or investment strategies to the individual, not the average.

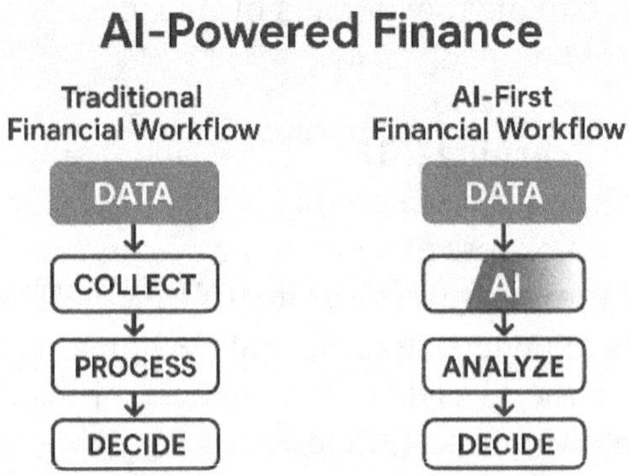

For SMB leaders, this means rethinking operations not around what humans can do faster—but around what AI can do smarter.

Real-World Use Cases Across Finance

AI is already embedded in financial workflows—often invisibly. Here are examples that directly impact small and mid-sized firms:

- **Credit Risk Modeling**: AI tools evaluate loan applicants using alternative data sources, improving access to capital for underbanked groups.
- **Invoice Fraud Detection**: Real-time analysis spots anomalies in billing patterns, flagging potentially fraudulent vendors.
- **Robo-Advisors**: Automated investment platforms lower the barrier to financial planning for smaller firms and their employees.

- **Claims Processing in Insurance**: AI speeds up claims by automatically interpreting images and forms, improving client trust.
- **RegTech (Regulatory Technology)**: AI reduces compliance burdens by flagging transactions that need manual review and generating audit-ready reports.

Real-World Example

What happened: A regional SMB-focused bank partnered with a fintech vendor to deploy an AI-powered underwriting system for small business loans.

What went right: Approval time dropped from 11 days to 3 hours. Defaults stayed within target range. Customer satisfaction increased dramatically.

What we learn: AI doesn't just cut costs—it transforms customer experience. Strategic deployment can outpace much larger competitors.

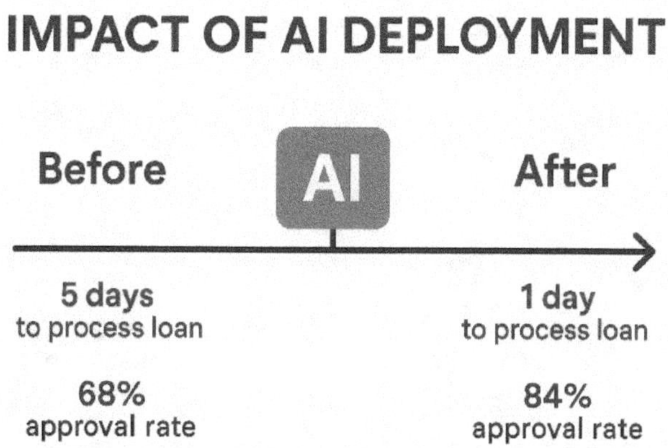

Global Trends and the Road to 2030

The financial AI wave isn't just a U.S. phenomenon. Worldwide, regulators, innovators, and customers are pushing the industry forward:

- **Europe**: GDPR and AI Act are setting privacy-aware AI governance standards that affect all financial firms.
- **Asia**: China and Singapore lead in AI-powered digital banking and cashless transactions.
- **Latin America**: Fintech adoption is skyrocketing, especially in credit scoring and mobile payments.

Forecasts indicate that by 2030:

- Over 80% of financial customer interactions will involve AI.
- AI will handle more than 60% of fraud detection and prevention activities.
- SMBs will represent the fastest-growing AI adoption segment in fintech.

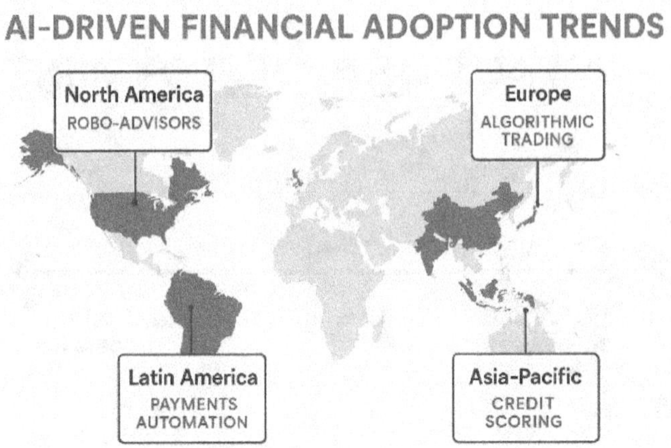

This isn't about distant predictions. It's about preparing your business to thrive in the next five years—not play catch-up in ten.

Conclusion

AI is reshaping finance from the inside out. For SMBs and forward-looking leaders, this is a moment to lead—because being small is no longer a disadvantage when AI levels the playing field.

What matters now is your strategy: understanding where AI fits, what risks it carries, and how to deploy it with precision.

Next Steps

- Audit your current workflows for repeatable, data-heavy tasks that could benefit from automation.
- Explore off-the-shelf AI tools from credible vendors that offer financial applications with minimal setup.
- Start small, but scale fast—pilot one use case, measure the ROI, then expand.
- Train your leadership team on AI literacy—understanding what it is, what it isn't, and how to govern it.

Next up: We move from the broad to the tactical. Chapter 2, *AI in Investment Decision-Making*, explores how machine learning is transforming portfolio strategy, risk models, and the very nature of financial advice.

Chapter 2: AI in Investment Decision-Making

AI is no longer just augmenting investment strategy—it's rewriting the rulebook. From hedge funds to retirement planners, the shift toward AI-driven decision-making is accelerating. For small and mid-sized investment firms or advisors, understanding how to leverage these tools can mean the difference between growth and irrelevance.

AI helps eliminate guesswork, uncover hidden patterns, and act on insights faster than any human team. But adopting it wisely requires a firm grasp on both its power and its limitations.

AI vs Traditional Portfolio Management

Traditional portfolio management often relies on human analysts using a mix of historical data, expert judgment, and fixed allocation models. While this approach has been serviceable for decades, it suffers from:

- Cognitive biases (recency bias, overconfidence)
- Slow adaptation to changing markets
- Limited ability to process large datasets

AI-powered systems, by contrast, are:

- **Data-Driven**: Able to analyze millions of variables in real time
- **Adaptive**: Continuously learning and evolving with market behavior
- **Objective**: Immune to emotion, media noise, or sleep deprivation

That doesn't mean replacing people—it means enhancing them. AI becomes the analyst's assistant, surfacing patterns, anomalies, and correlations no human could catch alone.

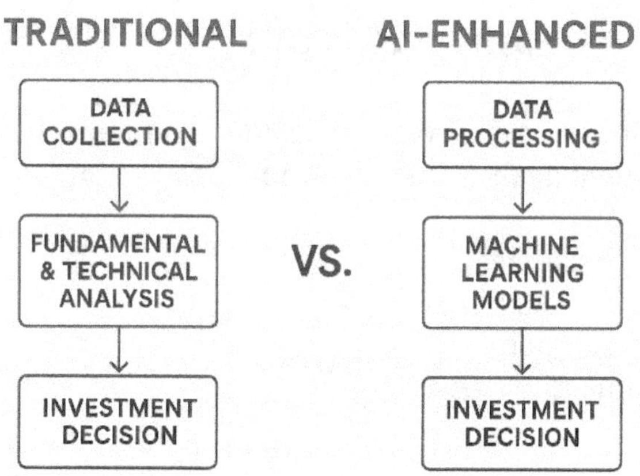

Portfolio Optimization with Machine Learning

Portfolio optimization is about maximizing return while managing risk. AI takes this further by:

- Predicting asset correlations more accurately in volatile markets
- Simulating market scenarios with dynamic variables
- Optimizing asset mixes across thousands of possible combinations

Key ML techniques used here include:

- **Reinforcement Learning**: Continuously improves portfolio choices through simulated trading environments
- **Bayesian Optimization**: Finds the most probable success paths under uncertainty
- **Clustering Algorithms**: Groups assets based on behavior rather than industry labels

These models aren't hypothetical—they're driving decisions inside robo-advisors, hedge funds, and increasingly, corporate treasuries.

Sentiment Analysis from Market Signals

Market sentiment often drives price more than fundamentals. AI-driven sentiment analysis uses NLP to digest:

- News headlines
- Social media posts
- Analyst reports
- Earnings call transcripts

This enables:

- Early detection of shifts in public perception
- Short-term trading signals
- Longer-term trend identification

SMBs using trading platforms can now access sentiment dashboards that once required a Bloomberg Terminal.

Real-World Example

What happened: A mid-sized asset manager integrated sentiment analysis into its equity screening process.

What went right: It caught early warning signals from tech sector news ahead of a downturn, allowing the firm to reduce exposure just in time.

What we learn: Sentiment isn't soft—it's actionable when processed correctly. AI turns noise into signal.

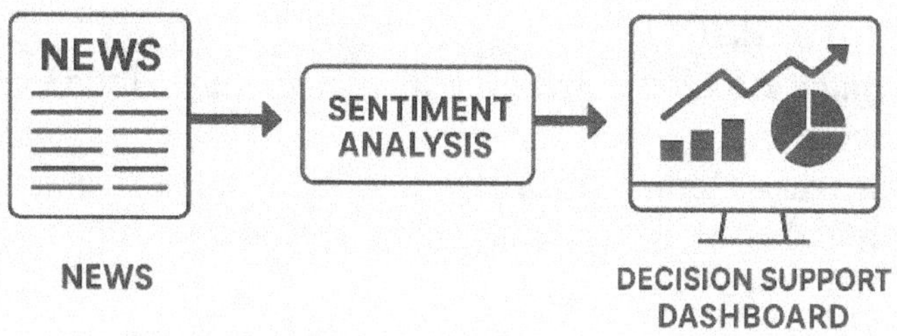

AI in Quantitative Funds

Quantitative funds—or "quant funds"—rely heavily on algorithmic models. AI takes this to a new level:

- Faster model iteration and backtesting
- Real-time adjustment to risk metrics
- Integration of alternative data (weather, shipping, satellite imagery)

These funds now outperform many traditional actively managed portfolios, particularly in volatile or niche markets.

SMB-focused quant tools are emerging too—allowing even small firms to build rules-based investment strategies powered by machine learning.

Risks & Ethical Concerns in Automated Investing

AI investing isn't without downside. Key risks include:

- **Overfitting**: Models that perform well on past data but fail in live markets
- **Black Box Risk**: Inability to explain why a model made a decision
- **Market Homogenization**: Too many actors using similar AI models can lead to herd behavior

Ethical issues also arise:

- **Bias**: Models trained on flawed data can reinforce inequalities
- **Access**: Wealthier firms may monopolize best AI tools, widening the gap
- **Accountability**: Who's to blame when an AI-driven decision causes a loss?

Checklist for SMB Investment Leaders:

- ☑ Clearly define human vs AI roles in investment strategy
- ☑ Vet all models for transparency and auditability
- ☑ Diversify AI tools—don't rely on a single vendor or signal
- ☑ Align AI outputs with fiduciary duty and compliance obligations

Conclusion

AI is not the future of investing—it's the present. Firms that adopt AI thoughtfully gain an edge in speed, scale, and insight. But that edge comes with a responsibility to manage complexity, mitigate bias, and maintain human judgment.

Next Steps

- Assess your current investment process for AI-ready components
- Partner with firms offering explainable, auditable AI tools
- Test sentiment and optimization tools in sandbox environments before going live
- Prepare your compliance team for AI oversight challenges

Next up: In Chapter 3, *Machine Learning for Risk Management*, we explore how predictive models can forecast credit risk, catch early warnings, and reduce exposure before losses hit.

Chapter 3: Machine Learning for Risk Management

Risk management is the backbone of financial resilience. Whether you're lending, investing, or underwriting, the ability to anticipate and absorb shocks defines your survivability. Machine learning has become the modern shield—faster, sharper, and more adaptive than traditional models.

But it's not about replacing risk officers with algorithms. It's about equipping them with predictive insight at a speed and scale no human team can match. For SMBs, this means real-time threat detection and smarter decisions without the overhead of enterprise analytics teams.

Credit Risk vs Market Risk: AI Use Cases

AI doesn't treat all risks the same—and neither should you. Different types of financial exposure require different models.

- **Credit Risk**: The danger that a borrower won't repay. ML models here analyze historical repayment patterns, alternative data (like utility bills or social behavior), and cash flow trends to assign dynamic credit scores.
- **Market Risk**: Exposure to shifts in interest rates, equity prices, currencies, or commodities. ML monitors global variables and simulates stress events with more nuance than static models.

Example Applications:

- Automating loan approval thresholds based on predicted default risk
- Rebalancing portfolios when volatility indicators spike
- Adjusting credit lines dynamically as risk signals change

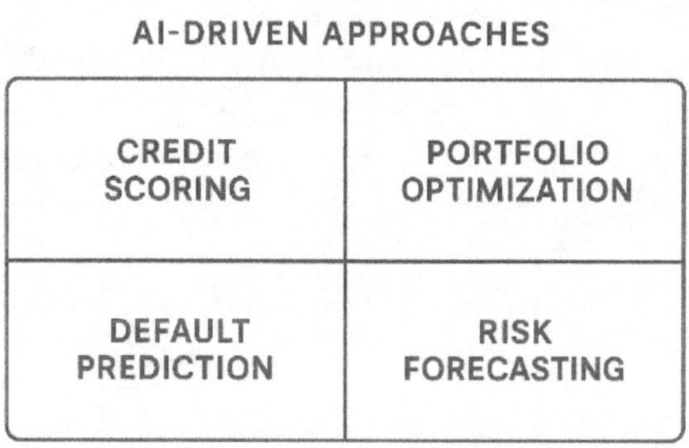

Predictive Risk Scoring Models

Traditional risk scoring models use fixed formulas and static inputs. ML-based models learn from trends and outcomes, improving accuracy over time. Key techniques include:

- **Gradient Boosted Trees**: Effective for tabular financial data, improving default predictions
- **Logistic Regression with Regularization**: Still useful when transparency is required, but with better tuning
- **Neural Nets**: For more complex patterns, especially when integrating diverse data types

Benefits:

- Higher accuracy in scoring
- Ability to factor in nonlinear relationships
- Continuous learning as new data arrives

Tactical Best Practices:

- ☑ Use hybrid models (ML + rule-based) for regulatory interpretability
- ☑ Regularly test for model drift—especially during volatile periods
- ☑ Maintain human override controls for outliers or flagged anomalies

Early Warning Systems with ML

The real value of AI is not just assessing risk—it's predicting when it's about to rise.

ML-driven early warning systems:

- Monitor real-time indicators (payment behavior, sentiment signals, geopolitical feeds)
- Trigger alerts before KPIs deteriorate
- Prioritize at-risk clients or assets for review

Real-World Example:

What happened: A mid-sized leasing firm deployed an ML-based early warning system across its client base.

What went right: The system flagged subtle delays in recurring payments by one segment. A deeper dive revealed exposure to a supplier in financial distress—months before formal credit downgrades occurred.

What we learn: ML didn't just prevent loss. It bought time. And time is leverage.

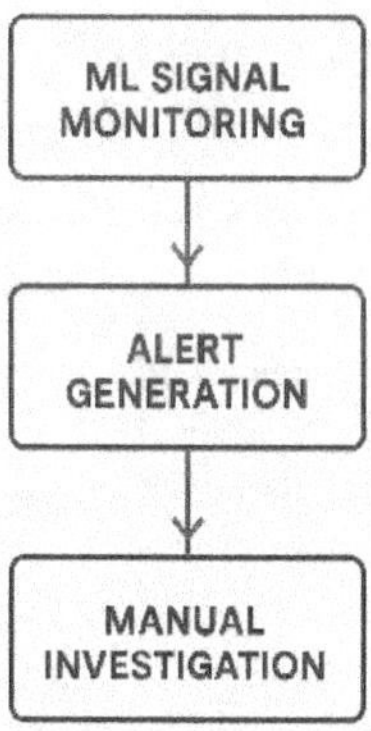

AI in Insurance Risk Modeling

Insurers are increasingly adopting ML to refine their core functions:

- **Underwriting**: ML enhances actuarial tables with behavioral and external data (driving history, IoT devices, climate models)
- **Pricing**: Dynamic adjustment of premiums based on real-time risk indicators
- **Claims**: Fraud detection through anomaly spotting and pattern analysis

For SMBs that underwrite or insure niche markets, AI levels the field. It enables fine-tuned pricing, faster assessments, and more profitable underwriting.

Common Pitfalls:

- Over-reliance on proxy data that lacks long-term predictive strength
- Ignoring regulatory pushback on opaque or discriminatory pricing models
- Failing to document explainability in AI underwriting decisions

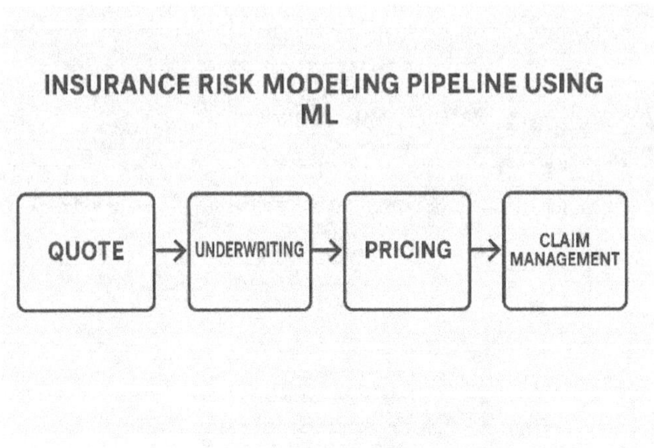

Limitations and Model Bias in Risk Forecasting

AI is powerful—but not perfect. Risk models are only as good as their data and design. Here's where most go wrong:

- **Training on the Wrong Historical Data**: Using data from low-volatility years to predict high-stress periods
- **Ignoring Feedback Loops**: Model-driven decisions that influence the environment, then reinforce biased outcomes
- **Overconfidence in Correlations**: Misreading causation leads to false confidence and exposure

Bias is another silent threat:

- Demographic bias in lending models
- Regional bias in insurance underwriting
- Confirmation bias from hand-labeled training data

Checklist for Ethical Risk Modeling:

- ☑ Run fairness audits across demographic slices
- ☑ Use adversarial testing to uncover hidden bias
- ☑ Document model assumptions and keep a versioned change log
- ☑ Involve human risk officers in regular model reviews

Conclusion

Machine learning can dramatically elevate your risk management capabilities—if you respect its boundaries. Used wisely, it empowers faster decisions, earlier warnings, and smarter underwriting. But if left unchecked, it can magnify blind spots.

The future of financial risk lies in the human-AI partnership: analysts armed with data-driven foresight and tools that serve, not replace, judgment.

Next Steps

- Review current risk models for signs of stagnation or overfitting
- Pilot an ML early warning system in one risk domain (credit, market, or insurance)
- Build governance into your model lifecycle—document, monitor, and review regularly
- Train your teams on interpreting AI risk scores, not just reading them

Coming up: Chapter 4, *Predictive Analytics in Stock Forecasting*, explores how AI-powered models are transforming market prediction—from time-series analysis to neural networks and real-time strategy engines.

Chapter 4: Predictive Analytics in Stock Forecasting

Stock forecasting is one of the most high-stakes, high-noise challenges in finance—and AI is now making measurable inroads into what was once thought to be a purely human judgment game. While no system can predict markets with certainty, AI brings tools that dramatically enhance signal detection, speed, and adaptability.

For small firms, this isn't about building the next hedge fund supercomputer. It's about intelligently leveraging models that turn raw data into better-informed trading and investment decisions. But effective use of AI in forecasting isn't about plugging in a model and expecting miracles—it's about understanding where the data comes from, how the models work, and how to interpret what they produce.

The Challenge of Stock Forecasting

Predicting market movements is hard for a reason. Prices are influenced not only by fundamentals (earnings, interest rates, global trade), but by human behavior: fear, greed, panic, speculation. This complexity is why traditional models have often failed in fast-changing markets.

AI doesn't eliminate uncertainty—but it improves your odds by:

- Identifying hidden patterns in massive, noisy datasets
- Updating strategies dynamically as new data flows in
- Reducing reaction time and cognitive overload in decision-making

SMBs that invest—or advise investors—can now access tools once locked inside proprietary trading desks. The key is using them responsibly.

Time-Series Modeling with AI

Time-series forecasting underpins everything from daily stock prices to interest rate trends. AI-enhanced models have outpaced legacy methods like ARIMA and exponential smoothing, offering:

- **Adaptability** to regime changes (e.g., pandemic-era volatility)
- **Context-aware forecasting**, where external events influence trajectory
- **Higher dimensionality**, using more variables than traditional models can handle

Advanced Time-Series Tools:

- **LSTM (Long Short-Term Memory) Networks**: Excellent for capturing long-term dependencies and nonlinear patterns.
- **Temporal Fusion Transformers (TFTs)**: These outperform LSTMs by combining time-series with contextual and static data.
- **Facebook Prophet**: While not pure AI, Prophet enables flexible modeling with holiday, trend, and seasonality inputs—ideal for smaller firms.

Tactical Best Practices:

- ☑ Always test on out-of-sample data
- ☑ Monitor for regime shifts (e.g., interest rate cycle changes)
- ☑ Layer technical indicators and sentiment as parallel inputs

Neural Networks for Price Prediction

Neural networks have evolved beyond academic curiosity. Today, they drive real decisions—especially in:

- **Short-term price movement forecasting**
- **Volatility prediction**
- **Market anomaly detection**

Real-World Neural Architectures:

- **Dense Feedforward Networks**: Useful for simple regression models
- **Convolutional Neural Networks (CNNs)**: Capture features from chart patterns
- **Autoencoders**: Reduce noise and highlight latent structures in complex inputs

Key Inputs Often Used:

- Price momentum indicators
- Order book dynamics
- Earnings call sentiment (via NLP)

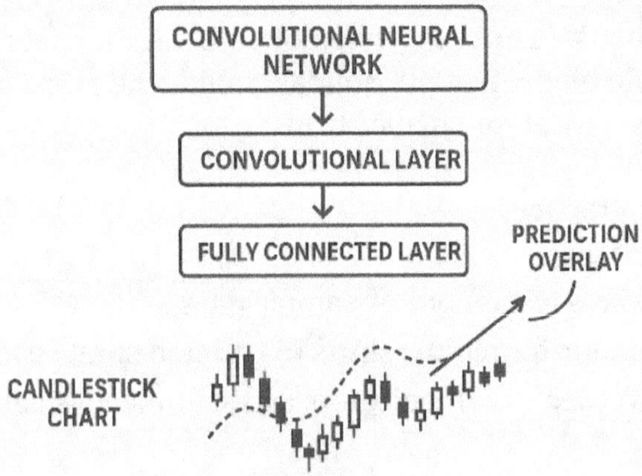

Common Pitfalls:

- Overfitting to short time windows
- Treating historical relationships as static truths
- Ignoring explainability for compliance purposes

Neural networks are powerful—but opaque. SMBs should use them with interpretability tools like SHAP or LIME to trace prediction logic.

Reinforcement Learning in Trading Strategy

Unlike supervised learning, reinforcement learning (RL) learns by doing—rewarding successful actions and penalizing poor ones in simulated markets.

In trading, an RL agent is trained to:

- Decide whether to buy, sell, or hold
- Adjust based on market feedback
- Improve profitability over thousands of episodes

Practical RL Strategies:

- **Q-Learning** for discrete action environments
- **Deep Deterministic Policy Gradient (DDPG)** for continuous strategies
- **Proximal Policy Optimization (PPO)** for robust and generalizable agents

SMBs can leverage RL in:

- ETF rebalancing with constraints (e.g., tax sensitivity)
- Options hedging strategies
- Dynamic stop-loss adjustment based on volatility bands

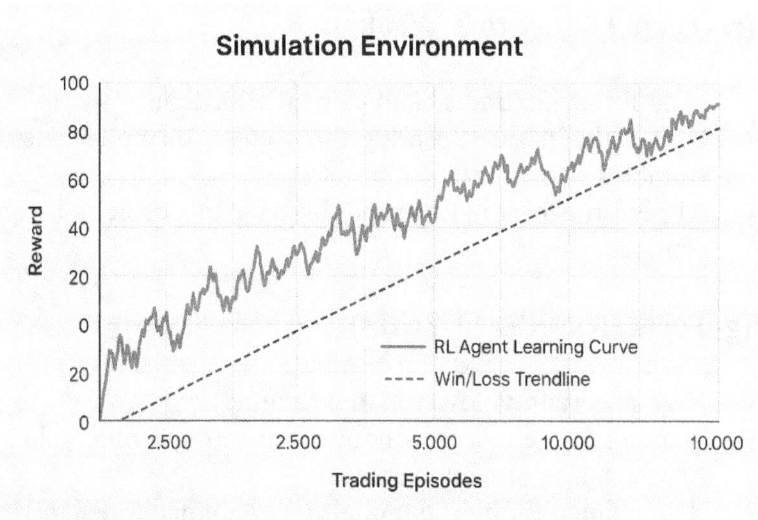

Checklist for Responsible RL Use:

- ☑ Define reward functions clearly—don't reward risk-taking blindly
- ☑ Train on simulated AND historical data
- ☑ Run adversarial testing—simulate shocks to test stability

Real-Time vs Long-Term Forecasting

The effectiveness of AI depends heavily on your time horizon. Misalignment between model design and decision window is a frequent failure point.

Real-Time (Intraday) Forecasting:

- Used by high-frequency traders
- Requires millisecond latency, tick-by-tick data
- Demands edge computing and co-location services

Short-Term (1 Day to 2 Weeks):

- Ideal for swing traders and tactical allocation
- Uses daily OHLC (open-high-low-close) data plus external variables
- AI performs best in this band due to manageable noise and actionable signals

Long-Term (Months to Years):

- High uncertainty, lower model accuracy
- Should include macroeconomic indicators, demographic trends, and sentiment averages
- Better suited for hybrid models (AI + human foresight)

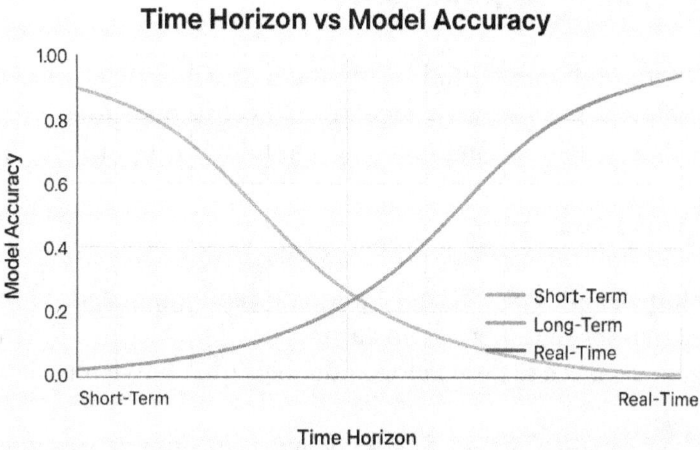

Tactical Insight:

Start short. Master short-term models, then layer macroeconomic elements for longer outlooks.

Hybrid Forecasting: Human vs AI

A growing body of research shows the most effective forecasting setups are **not fully automated**. Instead, they blend:

- Machine speed and pattern recognition
- Human context and qualitative filtering

What AI Does Better:

- Detect micro-patterns in large data sets
- Generate forecasts at scale (e.g., 10,000 assets)
- Identify non-obvious correlations (e.g., weather vs retail stock movement)

What Humans Still Do Better:

- Interpret unexpected geopolitical events
- Navigate regulatory, legal, or ethical implications
- Apply institutional memory and relationship-driven insight

Real-World Example:

What happened: A U.S.-based mid-cap fund integrated AI to analyze market sentiment from earnings call transcripts. Portfolio managers used the insights alongside their qualitative models.

What went right: The AI flagged negative sentiment from tech earnings before downgrades were issued. Fund managers trimmed exposure and preserved capital.

What we learn: Contextual AI isn't replacing intuition—it's enhancing it.

Data: The Fuel and the Filter

No forecasting model can outrun poor data. Stock prediction success is tightly bound to:

- **Data freshness**: Is your feed delayed? Your edge is gone.
- **Data integrity**: Are values accurate, complete, and unbiased?
- **Data diversity**: Are you incorporating external variables (weather, news sentiment, search trends)?

Tactical Data Sources:

- Financial APIs (IEX Cloud, Alpha Vantage, Quandl)
- News aggregators with NLP integration (Accern, Dataminr)
- Alternative data marketplaces (AWS Data Exchange, Crux)

SMBs should treat data infrastructure as a core competency—not a side project.

Explainability and Compliance

AI doesn't live in a vacuum. SMBs using predictive models must:

- Maintain audit trails of model predictions
- Explain forecasts to clients and regulators
- Document data lineage and transformation logic

Explainable AI (XAI) frameworks help here. Tools like:

- **SHAP (SHapley Additive exPlanations)**
- **LIME (Local Interpretable Model-Agnostic Explanations)**

These frameworks visualize which inputs drove which predictions, increasing trust.

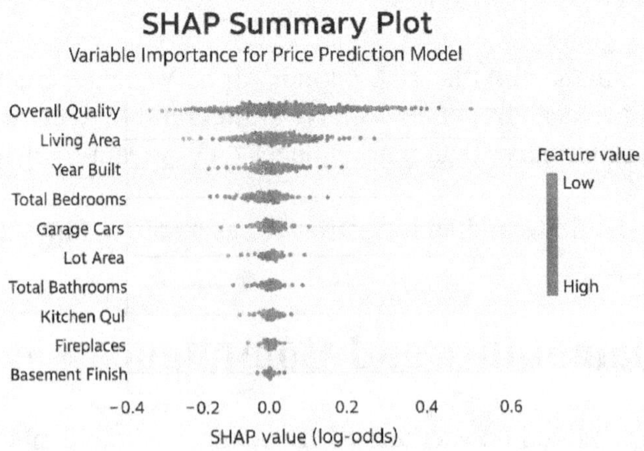

Checklist for Compliance Readiness:

- ☑ Document your AI pipeline, including training and test splits
- ☑ Include human review checkpoints in client-facing tools
- ☑ Store model versions and validation logs securely

Common Mistakes in AI Forecasting

- **Using too much data, too early**: More isn't always better
- **Ignoring latency and signal decay**: Yesterday's insight may be today's risk
- **Blindly trusting model performance metrics**: High backtest accuracy doesn't equal future profit

Fix them by:

- Starting lean—track a small set of KPIs and expand
- Testing against real-world slippage and costs
- Maintaining human override capacity

Conclusion

AI forecasting isn't magic—it's mathematics, speed, and constant iteration. For SMBs willing to build thoughtfully, it offers a serious edge in market visibility and risk management. But success depends on more than code: it requires good data, clear thinking, and a willingness to ask hard questions when models go wrong.

By blending human oversight with machine precision, forecasting becomes not just faster—but smarter.

Next Steps

- Evaluate your current forecasting processes—where are the blind spots?
- Choose a time horizon and match your model architecture accordingly
- Invest in diverse, high-quality data—not just more data
- Build interpretability into your AI stack from day one
- Pilot one AI model in a real-world scenario, measure ROI, then scale

Coming up: Chapter 5, *AI in Personal Finance and Robo-Advisors*, explores how automation and personalization are reshaping how individuals budget, invest, and plan their financial future—from voice assistants to regulatory friction.

Chapter 5: AI in Personal Finance and Robo-Advisors

For decades, personal finance was a relationship-driven field. Clients met with human advisors, discussed life goals, and received tailored advice—often delivered slowly and with significant cost. Today, that landscape is undergoing a historic transformation. Artificial intelligence is no longer reserved for hedge funds or enterprise fintech. It's powering the financial tools used by everyday consumers—and reshaping how people save, invest, spend, and plan.

This chapter explores how AI is redefining personal finance, from robo-advisors and personalized guidance to spending prediction and digital assistants. More importantly, it offers business leaders, consultants, and financial professionals insight into the real impact of these tools on behavior, trust, and regulation.

What Are Robo-Advisors?

A robo-advisor is a digital platform that provides automated, algorithm-driven financial planning services with little to no human supervision. These platforms ask users a series of questions—about risk tolerance, time horizon, financial goals—and then automatically build and manage an investment portfolio.

But the term "robo-advisor" undersells what these platforms have become. Today's systems are far more than rebalancing tools. They incorporate:

- **Machine learning algorithms** that adapt to economic shifts
- **Natural language interfaces** that let users engage via chat or voice
- **Behavioral analytics** that assess emotional investing patterns

Examples include:

- Wealthfront and Betterment for general investing
- Ellevest for gender-aware financial planning
- Acorns for micro-investing and round-ups

For SMBs, this matters for two reasons:

1. Your employees and clients increasingly use these tools
2. You can partner with or white-label robo-advisor tech to offer modern services

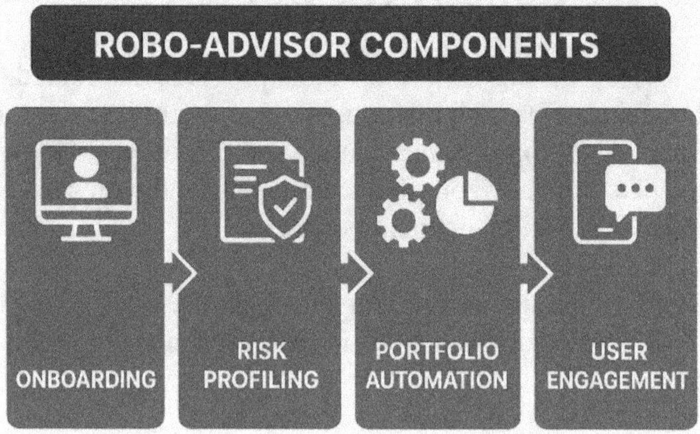

Personalized AI-Driven Investment Advice

The next wave of personal finance is hyper-personalization. AI systems can now tailor advice not just by age or income—but by behavior, transaction history, digital footprint, and even life stage events.

Key Personalization Features:

- **Dynamic Risk Profiling**: Adjusts based on behavior (e.g., panic-selling flags a more conservative risk tolerance)
- **Life Event Prediction**: Suggests financial moves based on detected milestones—like moving, marriage, or childbirth
- **Cash Flow Sensitivity**: Adapts investment plans if discretionary income drops or spikes

AI-powered advisors also integrate tax optimization, ESG preferences, and even charitable giving goals.

Real-World Use Case:

What happened: A robo-advisor for freelancers incorporated invoice timing and client payment habits into its algorithm.

What went right: Users experienced fewer overdrafts, better cash buffers, and more consistent savings.

What we learn: Personal finance AI works best when it understands income volatility—not just static inputs.

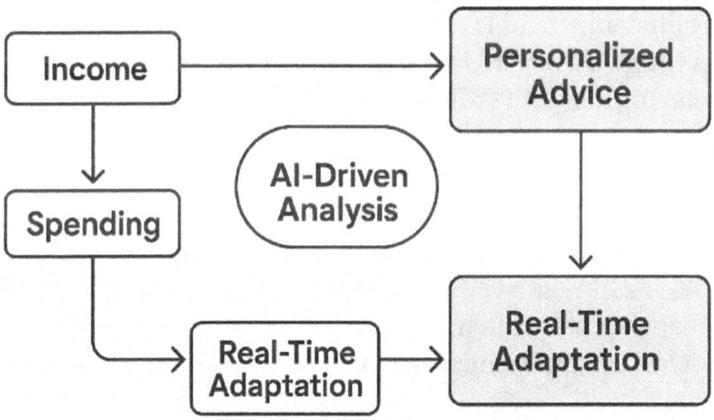

Tactical Best Practices for SMBs:

- ☑ If you offer financial benefits, integrate with robo platforms your employees already use
- ☑ Use AI-powered advisory as a value-add—not a threat—to human advisors
- ☑ Prioritize tools that disclose their personalization logic and adjustment triggers

Budgeting & Spending Prediction Tools

AI-driven budgeting isn't about charts and pie graphs—it's about prediction and intervention. These tools go beyond showing past behavior to actively forecasting future patterns and nudging behavior change.

What Modern Tools Can Do:

- **Predict Upcoming Expenses**: Based on seasonality, subscriptions, and prior behavior
- **Flag Risky Trends**: Identifies if discretionary spending is outpacing income
- **Nudge Toward Goals**: Suggests micro-adjustments to meet savings or debt reduction targets

Examples:

- Cleo: Chat-based assistant with predictive analytics
- YNAB (You Need A Budget): Behavioral AI integrations for habit reinforcement
- Mint with machine learning add-ons (subscription tier)

Checklist for SMB Relevance:

- ☑ Offer or recommend predictive tools to employees for financial wellness
- ☑ Use spending pattern forecasts in customer credit risk modeling
- ☑ Evaluate vendors based on privacy and user data control

Common Pitfalls:

- Assuming all users spend consistently—ML must adapt to outliers
- Over-focusing on averages—real life is lumpy
- Neglecting emotional spending triggers (stress, holidays, bonuses)

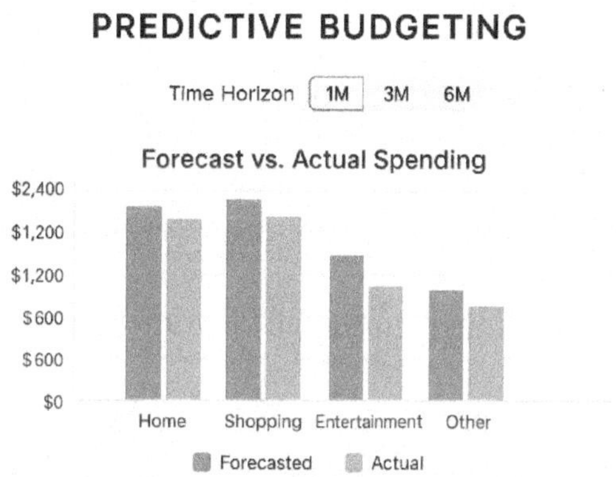

Voice & Chat Assistants in Personal Finance

Conversational AI is becoming the user interface for finance. Today's customers want hands-free control, quick answers, and natural interactions—not portals filled with menus.

Applications Include:

- **Balance Inquiries & Spending Summaries**: Delivered via Alexa, Google Assistant, or in-app chat
- **Transaction Categorization**: "What was that $187 charge on my Visa?"
- **Goal Progress Updates**: "How close am I to my emergency fund target?"

More advanced systems also:

- Recognize financial jargon
- Distinguish voice tones for stress indicators
- Escalate to human reps when confusion or urgency is detected

For SMBs offering financial products, this means:

- ☑ Design support flows for chat and voice from the start
- ☑ Train assistants on your specific terminology, products, and support history
- ☑ Monitor user sentiment and frustration signals—these are early churn predictors

Real-World Example:

What happened: A regional credit union integrated a bilingual chat assistant trained in common financial questions.

What went right: Member support tickets dropped by 38%. Users rated chat satisfaction higher than phone support.

What we learn: Voice and chat AI aren't about novelty—they're about accessibility and scale.

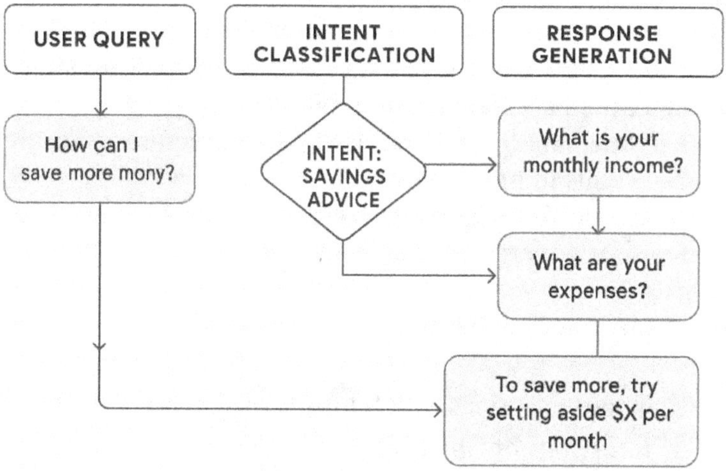

Consumer Trust, Regulation, and Adoption Trends

Even the most powerful AI in personal finance will fail if users don't trust it. Trust is earned through clarity, control, and consistency.

Key Trust Factors:

- **Explainability**: Users want to know why the AI made a suggestion
- **Control**: They need to feel they can override or customize automation
- **Privacy**: How is their data collected, stored, and used?

Regulatory Trends:

- **U.S.**: CFPB has flagged AI-based credit decisions for potential bias and lack of explainability
- **Europe**: GDPR and proposed AI Act require transparency and rights to human review
- **Asia-Pacific**: Singapore MAS promotes AI in finance but requires governance and fairness audits

Tactical Compliance Actions:

- ☑ Choose vendors with built-in consent and privacy modules
- ☑ Keep logs of financial decisions made or influenced by AI
- ☑ Implement opt-out features for personalization or automation

Adoption Trends by Demographic:

- Gen Z and Millennials adopt AI tools rapidly—especially mobile-first ones
- Gen X trusts hybrid models (human + AI)
- Boomers show highest demand for explainability and human fallback

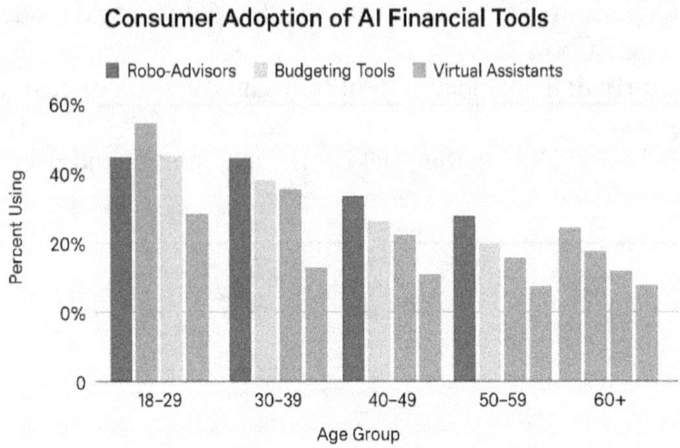

Real-World Pitfall Scenario

What happened: A fintech startup offered AI-powered savings nudges but didn't disclose that withdrawals were temporarily restricted after savings moves.

What went wrong: Social media backlash erupted. Trust eroded. Regulatory attention followed.

What we learn: Automating finances is a privilege. It demands transparency, frictionless opt-outs, and sensitivity to real-life liquidity needs.

Conclusion

AI is redefining personal finance—from how advice is delivered to how spending is predicted. For SMBs, fintechs, and advisors, the opportunity is massive—but only if the technology respects trust, autonomy, and clarity.

AI doesn't make money decisions for people. It removes friction so they can make better ones. Done right, it builds financial confidence at scale.

Next Steps

- Audit your employee or customer financial tools—are they AI-enabled?
- Identify one area (budgeting, advisory, or support) where conversational AI could improve experience
- Choose tools that are explainable, privacy-conscious, and behaviorally aware
- Prepare for regulatory audits by logging decisions and user opt-ins

Up next: Chapter 6, *NLP for Financial News & Insights*, dives into how language models are transforming market signal detection, earnings call interpretation, and the future of real-time financial intelligence.

Chapter 6: NLP for Financial News & Insights

Financial decisions are increasingly driven by fast-moving, unstructured information—news headlines, earnings call transcripts, analyst reports, and social media chatter. The ability to extract insights from that flood of text has become a strategic advantage. This is where natural language processing (NLP) is changing the game.

For small and mid-sized financial firms, NLP was once out of reach. But with recent advances in pre-trained language models, real-time sentiment engines, and off-the-shelf APIs, powerful textual analysis is now accessible, scalable, and practical. This chapter explains how NLP converts language into action—from real-time news signals to executive-ready summaries—and why misinterpretation, bias, and context still demand human oversight.

How NLP Converts News into Signals

The financial press moves markets. But most firms still rely on manual monitoring or basic keyword alerts. NLP automates the transformation of headlines and articles into structured data signals.

NLP Pipeline in Finance:

1. **Text Ingestion**: Scrape or stream headlines from financial news sources
2. **Preprocessing**: Clean the text, remove noise, resolve named entities (companies, people, tickers)
3. **Classification**: Assign topics or event categories (e.g., "M&A activity" or "earnings beat")
4. **Sentiment Scoring**: Quantify tone as positive, neutral, or negative
5. **Signal Generation**: Convert NLP output into trading or alert signals

Popular tools include:

- RavenPack and Accern (news analytics platforms)
- Python libraries like spaCy, NLTK, or Hugging Face Transformers
- Custom models trained on finance-specific corpora

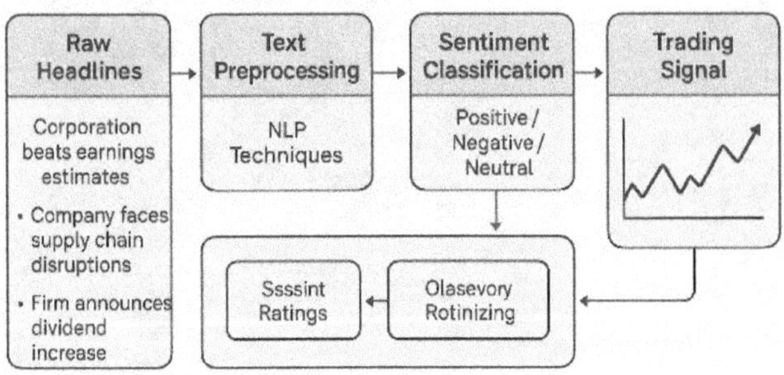

Real-World Application:

What happened: A boutique equity fund subscribed to a live NLP news feed that tagged M&A activity and market reactions.

What went right: The firm began detecting acquisition rumors hours ahead of formal releases, improving short-term positioning.

What we learn: Speed isn't enough—structured understanding is the edge.

Sentiment Analysis for Market Reaction

Sentiment drives short-term volatility. NLP enables real-time scanning of investor emotion embedded in news, social media, and analyst commentary.

Sentiment Inputs:

- News headlines
- Twitter and Reddit financial communities
- SEC filings and company press releases

Sentiment Outputs:

- **Polarity**: Positive, neutral, or negative
- **Intensity**: Strength of the sentiment
- **Targeted Subjects**: Which company or asset the sentiment applies to

Financial NLP models differ from generic ones. For example, "downgrade" in finance has a specific implication vs general speech. Misclassifying such terms can distort signals.

Term	Sentiment Polarity	Confidence
Profit growth	Positive	0.94
Downgrade	Negative	0.88
Strong demand	Positive	0.91
Bankruptcy	Negative	0.97
Revenue	Neutral	0.79
Risk exposure	Negative	0.89
Weak outlook	Negative	0.93
Beating expectations	Positive	0.85

Best Practices for SMB Use:

- ☑ Use industry-tuned sentiment models—generic NLP is too noisy
- ☑ Combine sentiment with volume or volatility data for context
- ☑ Validate against actual price movement to filter false positives

Earnings Call Analysis with Large Language Models

Earnings calls are rich in tone, subtext, and implication. Human analysts struggle to track thousands each quarter. Large language models (LLMs) now summarize and extract key insights in minutes.

What LLMs Can Do:

- Extract key themes (growth, margin pressure, guidance)
- Detect shifts in executive tone or evasiveness
- Compare current vs prior call language ("tone drift")

Popular tools:

- OpenAI GPT-based summarizers
- BERT fine-tuned on earnings data
- AlphaSense and Amenity Analytics

Real-World Use Case:

What happened: An SMB-focused fund used an LLM to scan 120 earnings calls in two days—something that previously took a full-time analyst two weeks.

What went right: The team flagged guidance downgrades faster than competitors and repositioned accordingly.

What we learn: Speed and depth aren't mutually exclusive when LLMs are used correctly.

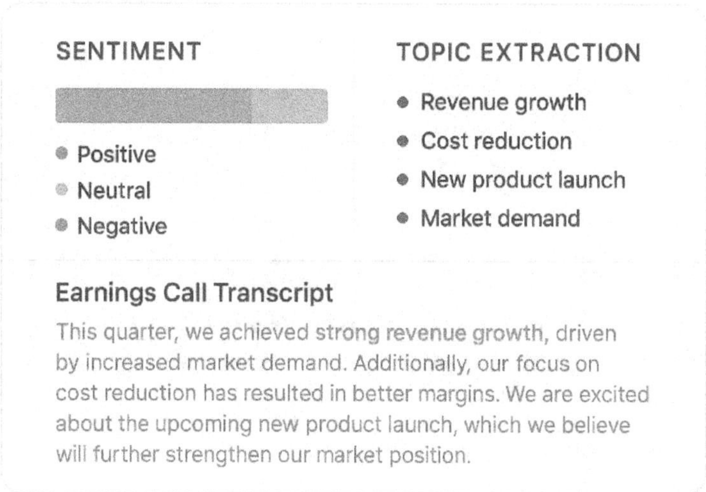

AI Summary Tools for Financial Briefs

Executives and clients don't want full reports—they want clarity. NLP summarization tools condense complex text into bite-sized insights without losing meaning.

Applications:

- **Portfolio Updates**: Summarize fund activity and outlook
- **Regulatory News**: Reduce 40-page reports to 5-line digests
- **Internal Briefings**: Condense analyst notes for leadership

Types of Summarization:

- **Extractive**: Pulls key sentences
- **Abstractive**: Rephrases and paraphrases key ideas

Checklist for Effective Use:

- ☑ Choose domain-specific summarizers where possible
- ☑ Manually validate summaries for high-stakes documents
- ☑ Include source links to original content for transparency

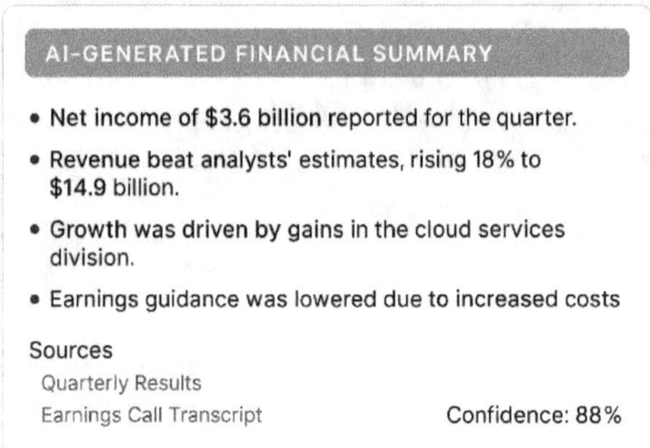

Bias & Misinterpretation in Financial NLP

Despite its power, NLP has limitations—and risks.

Key Risks:

- **Domain Drift**: Models trained on general corpora often misinterpret finance-specific context
- **Sentiment Bias**: Certain sectors (e.g., crypto, energy) attract emotionally loaded language
- **Misclassification**: Words like "drop" or "surge" may be misread without numeric anchors

Real-World Pitfall:

What happened: A social sentiment model flagged positive buzz for a retail stock during earnings week. But the volume spike came from sarcastic memes, not investor enthusiasm.

What went wrong: The model lacked sarcasm detection and failed to interpret contextual tone.

What we learn: NLP without nuance is noise.

Tactical Risk Mitigation:

- ☑ Use ensemble models to cross-check interpretations
- ☑ Manually review anomalies before acting
- ☑ Regularly retrain models on updated financial text sets

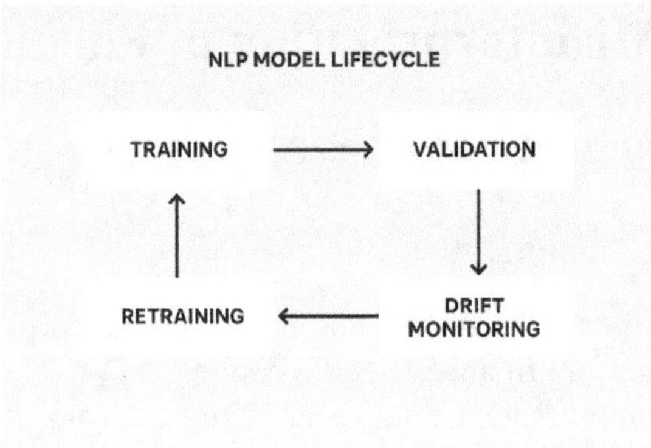

Conclusion

NLP is transforming how financial professionals interpret language. Whether it's turning news into data, summarizing earnings calls, or detecting sentiment shifts, the ability to structure text at scale delivers real-world performance gains.

But NLP is not a plug-and-play solution. Context, calibration, and oversight are critical—especially when the wrong interpretation can lead to financial loss or reputational risk.

For SMBs, NLP is no longer out of reach. The key is to start small, validate continuously, and always pair models with experienced human judgment.

Next Steps

- Audit your current use of unstructured data—where are the gaps?
- Identify one NLP use case (e.g., earnings call summaries, sentiment alerts) to pilot
- Choose a tool tuned to financial language—not generic NLP
- Build explainability and validation into every output stream

Up next: Chapter 7, *Fraud Detection with AI*, explores how machine learning identifies anomalies, prevents financial loss, and powers the next generation of real-time fraud defense systems.

Chapter 7: Fraud Detection with AI

Fraud is not a question of if—it's a question of when. In financial services, fraud is a constantly evolving threat that drains revenue, erodes trust, and invites regulatory scrutiny. But modern fraud is fast, sophisticated, and often invisible to rule-based systems. That's where artificial intelligence steps in.

AI-powered fraud detection doesn't just flag anomalies—it learns patterns, adapts to new attack vectors, and detects the subtle behavioral fingerprints of fraudulent activity. This chapter dives deep into how AI is transforming fraud prevention across sectors, from banking to insurance to credit cards, and what this means for SMBs looking to strengthen their defenses without breaking their budgets.

Types of Financial Fraud AI Detects

Fraud is not monolithic. It manifests differently depending on the sector and transaction type. AI tools are especially effective in detecting:

- **Transaction Fraud**: Unauthorized credit card or wire transfers
- **Application Fraud**: Fake accounts, synthetic identities, forged documentation
- **Insider Fraud**: Employee misuse of access or data
- **Claims Fraud**: In insurance, inflated or staged claims
- **Account Takeover**: Login compromise through phishing, credential stuffing, or malware

Each type has different data patterns. AI models trained on domain-specific fraud datasets outperform generalist detection systems.

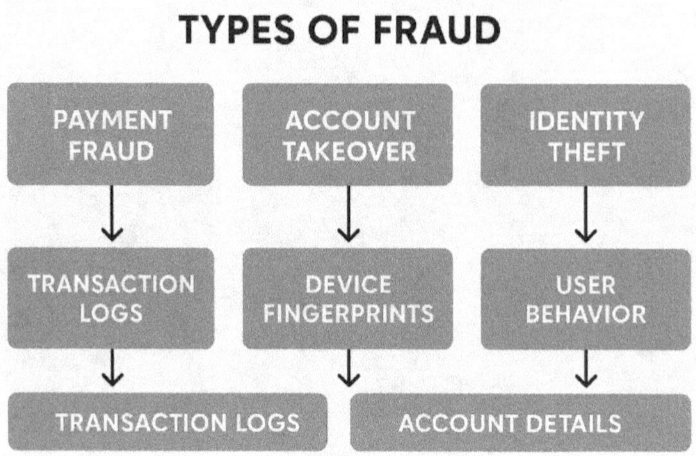

Pattern Recognition and Behavioral Analysis

Traditional fraud systems rely on static rules: "Flag any transaction over $5,000 from a foreign IP." But fraudsters adapt. AI systems look beyond fixed thresholds to understand behavior.

Key Techniques:

- **Anomaly Detection**: Identifies deviations from typical user behavior (e.g., spending time, location, device)
- **Behavioral Biometrics**: Measures how a person types, swipes, or navigates an app
- **Clustering Algorithms**: Groups user profiles to detect outliers
- **Sequence Modeling**: Uses time-series data to detect unnatural action sequences (e.g., login → password change → fund transfer within seconds)

Real-World Example:

What happened: A mid-sized digital wallet company deployed a behavioral ML model to track customer navigation and typing patterns.

What went right: They reduced account takeover incidents by 42% in six months. Legitimate users had seamless access, while bad actors were blocked in real time.

What we learn: Behavior is harder to fake than credentials.

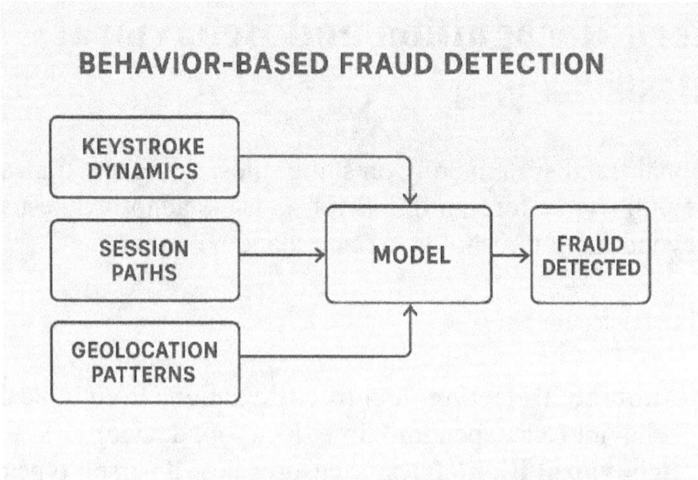

Real-Time Threat Detection with ML

Speed is critical in fraud detection. AI enables systems to operate in real time, rather than batch-mode post-incident analysis.

Features of Real-Time AI Systems:

- **Stream Processing**: Data is evaluated as it flows in
- **Low-Latency Models**: Deliver responses within milliseconds
- **Auto-Action Capabilities**: Trigger freezes, alerts, or step-up authentication automatically

Best Practices:

- ☑ Prioritize explainability—even in fast models
- ☑ Use confidence thresholds to reduce false positives
- ☑ Design escalation paths for edge cases

Checklist for SMB Deployment:

- ☑ Choose vendors with proven sub-second response benchmarks
- ☑ Integrate fraud scoring into customer experience flows (e.g., checkout, login)
- ☑ Monitor model drift—fraud evolves, and your models must too

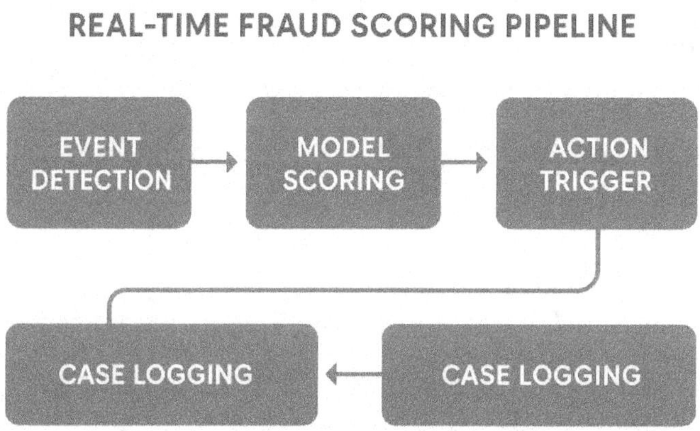

AI for Insurance & Credit Card Fraud

Fraud in insurance and payments requires specialized tools. Here's how AI supports each:

Insurance:

- **Image Analysis**: Detects altered or staged accident photos
- **Text NLP**: Flags inconsistent language in claims
- **Claim Pattern Clustering**: Identifies repeat fraud rings using shared addresses, phone numbers, or repair shops

Credit Cards:

- **Graph Neural Networks**: Track relationships between merchants, accounts, and devices
- **Device Fingerprinting**: Combines hardware and browser signals to flag new or suspicious setups
- **Velocity Checks**: ML-enhanced rules monitor rapid spend, merchant hopping, or geo-drift

Real-World Use Case:

What happened: An insurer integrated NLP and image recognition to scan incoming auto claims.

What went right: False claim detection improved 31%. Investigation costs dropped. Honest customers experienced faster approval.

What we learn: AI doesn't just prevent fraud—it protects customer experience.

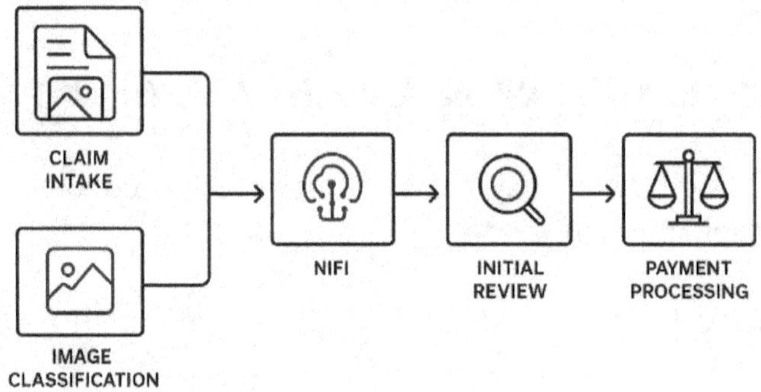

Insurance Claim Processing Pipeline enhancad
with image Classification at Intake stage

Success Stories in Financial Fraud Prevention

Success in AI fraud detection isn't about perfect prediction—it's about measurable reduction in impact, with minimal friction for genuine users.

Case 1: Mid-Sized Neobank

- **Problem**: Frequent card-present fraud at gas stations
- **Solution**: Deployed geolocation-based AI to cross-check card and mobile device position
- **Result**: Fraud losses cut by $1.2M in Q1. Customer complaints dropped 22%.

Case 2: Regional Insurer

- **Problem**: Staged injury claims using repeat actors
- **Solution**: ML cross-referenced claimant names, treatment clinics, and claim language
- **Result**: Identified a fraud ring operating across three states. Filed charges.

Case 3: SMB Fintech

- **Problem**: Synthetic identity applications for lines of credit
- **Solution**: Used ensemble models combining device history, velocity checks, and document forgery detection
- **Result**: Denied $4M in fraudulent credit within 90 days of deployment

Common Pitfalls in AI Fraud Systems

- **Overfitting to Historical Fraud**: Today's attacks may look different
- **Undertraining for Rare Events**: Fraud is rare—models need techniques like SMOTE or anomaly-boosting
- **False Positives**: A blocked transaction isn't just data—it's a lost customer
- **Poor Escalation Paths**: Flagging risk without human follow-up leads to missed or mishandled cases

Remedies:

- ☑ Use semi-supervised learning when labeled data is scarce
- ☑ Blend rules with models for layered defense
- ☑ Design clear handoffs from model → analyst → action

Conclusion

AI is redefining what's possible in fraud detection. With speed, adaptability, and behavior-based insights, it delivers protection that static systems can't match. But AI isn't magic—it requires training, monitoring, and strong human-in-the-loop design.

For SMBs, adopting AI for fraud is no longer optional. It's how you protect margins, customers, and your reputation in a landscape where fraudsters evolve daily.

Next Steps

- Identify your highest-risk fraud vectors—where do losses cluster?
- Assess whether your current fraud stack supports real-time analysis
- Pilot one AI model in a narrow domain (e.g., login risk, claim reviews)
- Monitor KPIs like false positive rate, fraud loss reduction, and investigation time

Up next: Chapter 8, *AI in Credit Scoring and Lending*, explores how alternative data, machine learning underwriting, and fairness frameworks are reshaping access to capital across industries.

Chapter 8: AI in Credit Scoring and Lending

Access to credit is a cornerstone of economic opportunity—but for decades, it's also been a gatekeeper. Traditional credit scoring models are rigid, exclusionary, and often blind to financial nuance. Artificial intelligence is upending this dynamic. By unlocking new data sources and learning from behaviors rather than static rules, AI is transforming how lenders assess risk, underwrite loans, and broaden financial access.

This chapter explores how AI is reshaping credit scoring and lending: what's replacing the legacy systems, how alternative data is fueling decisions, and what fairness, explainability, and compliance must look like in this new paradigm.

Traditional vs AI-Based Credit Models

Credit scores like FICO and VantageScore have long dominated lending decisions. These models rely heavily on:

- Credit utilization
- Payment history
- Length of credit history
- Types of credit accounts
- Inquiries

But these systems:

- Penalize thin-file or credit-invisible consumers
- Lag behind life changes (e.g., sudden income loss)
- Struggle to adjust for non-traditional income sources

AI-Based Models:

Machine learning models can:

- Analyze a broader range of financial behaviors
- Identify subtle patterns correlated with repayment likelihood
- Continuously improve with new data inputs

Types of AI models used:

- **Gradient Boosting Machines (GBMs)**: High-performing with structured data
- **Random Forests**: Effective for tabular credit data
- **Neural Networks**: Capture nonlinear interactions in large feature sets

	Traditional Credit Scoring	AI-Based Models
Data Inputs	Credit history, Income, Debt levels	Alternative data, Transaction patterns
Update Frequency	Periodic	Continuous
Fairness	Potential bias Limited transparency	Bias mitigation Explainability
Coverage	Established borrowers	Thin-credit and unbanked

For SMB lenders and fintechs, AI enables a more dynamic, inclusive, and accurate credit decisioning process.

Use of Alternative Data for Lending

Alternative data refers to information not traditionally used in credit scoring. This includes:

- Rent, utility, and telecom payment history
- Bank account cash flow
- Gig economy earnings
- Mobile phone usage patterns
- Social signals (when privacy-compliant)

Why It Matters:

Millions of consumers—especially younger, underbanked, or immigrant populations—have limited credit file data but demonstrate financial responsibility in other ways.

AI makes it possible to:

- Integrate diverse data formats
- Assign predictive weight to new signals
- Reduce bias toward privileged financial profiles

Real-World Use Case:

What happened: A micro-lender in Southeast Asia used mobile top-up history and location stability as underwriting criteria.

What went right: Loan repayment rates outperformed those based on legacy credit bureau scores.

What we learn: Responsible borrowing behavior shows up in everyday life—not just in credit card records.

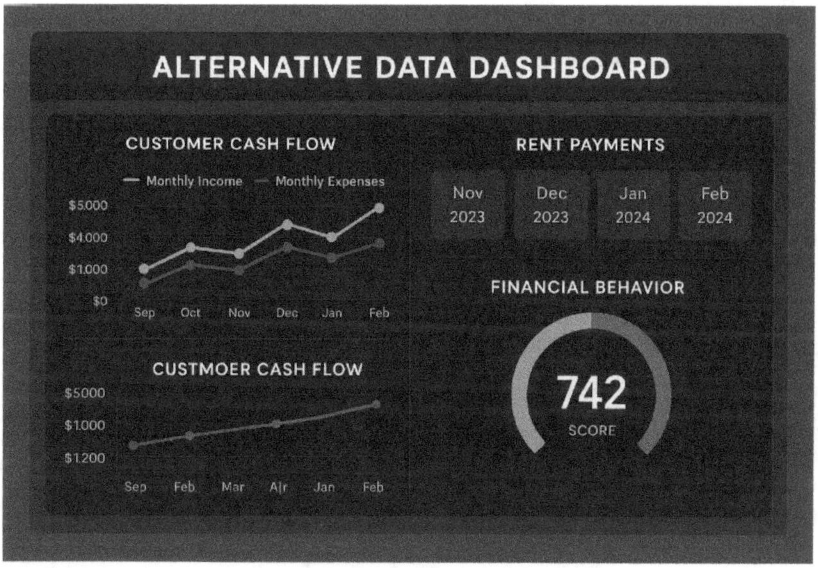

AI-Enhanced Underwriting Platforms

Modern underwriting platforms integrate AI to automate, accelerate, and refine loan decisioning.

Core Components:

- **Data Ingestion Engine**: Pulls in structured and unstructured data
- **Scoring Models**: Assign risk probabilities using supervised learning
- **Decision Rules Layer**: Overlay of business logic and regulatory constraints
- **Audit & Logging Interface**: Records every step for transparency

SMBs and community lenders can now:

- Reduce loan processing time from days to minutes
- Serve non-traditional borrowers without increasing risk
- Automate compliance reporting

Checklist for Adoption:

- ☑ Ensure API access to income verification and bank account data
- ☑ Use explainable AI (XAI) tools to support compliance
- ☑ Define override and appeal processes for declined applications

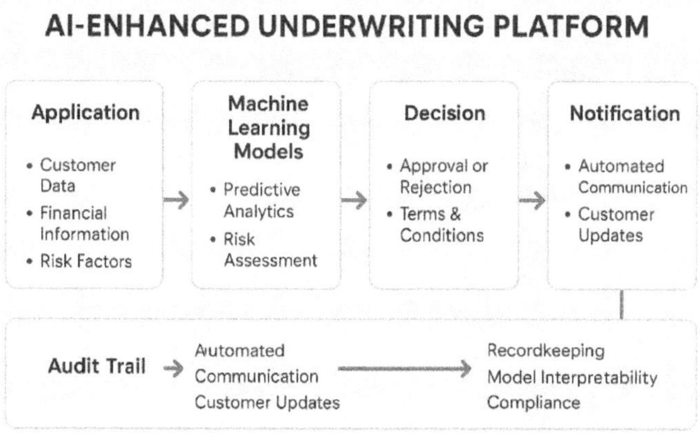

Fairness, Bias & Transparency Challenges

AI in lending offers opportunity—but also risk. Without proper governance, models can entrench discrimination under a veneer of automation.

Common Risks:

- **Proxy Bias**: Zip code used as a proxy for race
- **Historical Data Bias**: Training models on legacy approvals that were themselves biased
- **Opacity**: Inability to explain why a model made a specific lending decision

Regulatory Pressure:

- **U.S.**: Fair Lending laws, ECOA, and CFPB scrutiny
- **EU**: GDPR rights to explanation and non-discrimination
- **Global**: ISO/IEC standards emerging for ethical AI

Mitigation Tactics:

- ☑ Run fairness audits across protected classes
- ☑ Regularly reweight training data to balance outcomes
- ☑ Use counterfactual analysis to test if different decisions would occur for similar profiles

Real-World Pitfall:

What happened: A fintech's credit model had 25% higher rejection rates for female applicants due to historical income weighting.

What went wrong: Income was over-relied upon as a signal; it ignored self-employed and maternity income gaps.

What we learn: Bias isn't just unethical—it's also a business risk.

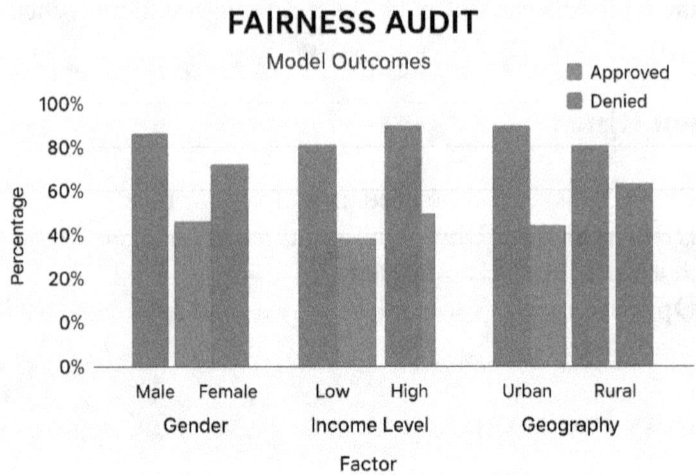

Financial Inclusion through AI Lending

One of AI's most promising impacts is expanding credit access to previously excluded groups. By moving beyond legacy scoring:

- Entrepreneurs with irregular income can qualify
- Immigrants and expats with no credit file can build financial identity
- Young adults can access credit earlier, based on real behavior

AI-driven inclusion initiatives:

- **India's Aadhaar-linked lending**
- **Latin America's WhatsApp-based loan origination**
- **U.S. community banks using bank cash flow analysis**

Real-World Example:

What happened: A U.S. CDFI (community development financial institution) used open banking data to approve auto loans for low-income borrowers.

What went right: Loan defaults remained within 2%, while approval rates jumped 38%.

What we learn: Inclusion doesn't mean higher risk—when the models are smart.

Conclusion

AI is transforming credit from a backward-looking, rigid system into a forward-thinking, inclusive decision engine. But with great power comes new responsibility. SMBs and fintechs must balance opportunity with accountability, ensuring that AI-driven lending is not only fast and scalable—but fair, explainable, and compliant.

The future of credit isn't about one score—it's about continuous insight, deeper data, and better questions.

Next Steps

- Review your current lending and credit scoring process—what's static or exclusionary?
- Identify an alternative data source (cash flow, utility data) to pilot
- Select an AI underwriting platform with explainability and audit features
- Run a fairness audit before and after deployment
- Prepare for transparency demands from both customers and regulators

Coming up next: Chapter 9, *Algorithmic Trading & HFT*, examines how AI and deep learning are powering microsecond-level trades, arbitrage, and execution optimization—alongside the regulatory risks of speed.

Chapter 9: Algorithmic Trading & HFT

Algorithmic trading and high-frequency trading (HFT) have transformed modern markets from a human-paced environment into an ultra-fast, AI-powered ecosystem. The integration of artificial intelligence into these systems has brought unmatched speed, precision, and analytical capability—but also increased complexity and regulatory scrutiny.

For SMBs, hedge funds, or trading firms stepping into the algo trading world, AI is a differentiator. It enhances execution, reduces slippage, and identifies market opportunities invisible to conventional tools. But as machines compete in microseconds, the risks—both technical and ethical—require equally sophisticated controls.

This chapter breaks down the building blocks of AI-powered algorithmic trading, explores deep learning in market microstructure, and provides clarity on where AI adds value—and where it must be reined in.

Overview of Algorithmic & High-Frequency Trading

Algorithmic trading refers to using rules-based software to execute trades based on predefined criteria. These criteria might include timing, price, volume, or external indicators. **High-Frequency Trading** is a subcategory that executes a large number of orders at extremely high speeds—often microseconds apart—capitalizing on minuscule price movements.

Core Characteristics:

- **Speed**: HFT systems operate at microsecond latency using co-located servers
- **Automation**: Decision-making is fully automated with minimal human intervention
- **Volume**: HFT firms may execute tens of thousands of trades per second

AI enhances these systems by:

- Predicting market behavior
- Optimizing execution timing and order routing
- Detecting short-lived arbitrage opportunities

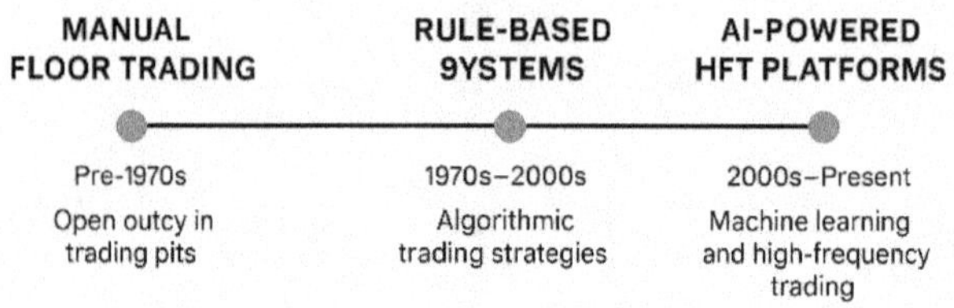

Deep Learning in Microstructure Analysis

Market microstructure deals with how trading occurs at the most granular level: order book dynamics, bid-ask spreads, latency arbitrage, and execution costs. Deep learning models provide significant advantages in this arena.

Key Deep Learning Techniques:

- **Recurrent Neural Networks (RNNs)**: Ideal for analyzing temporal sequences of order book data
- **Convolutional Neural Networks (CNNs)**: Applied to market depth visualizations to detect emerging patterns
- **Transformers**: Used to process multiple streams of market data in parallel

Input Signals for Microstructure Models:

- Level II order book snapshots
- Trade execution timestamps
- Liquidity metrics and queue positioning

Real-World Application:

What happened: A quant fund used a CNN trained on order book images to detect quote stuffing activity and avoid liquidity traps.

What went right: Trade execution quality improved by 15%, and slippage on large trades dropped.

What we learn: Micro-pattern recognition at the millisecond level can have macro-scale performance impact.

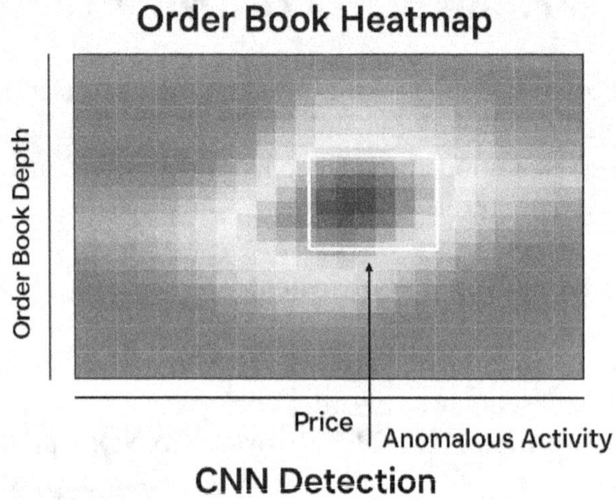

AI for Execution Optimization & Risk Control

AI isn't just about strategy—it plays a critical role in trade execution. With market conditions changing millisecond to millisecond, intelligent execution algorithms adapt in real time to maximize efficiency.

Functions of Execution AI:

- **Smart Order Routing (SOR)**: Chooses the optimal venue for best price and lowest latency
- **Slippage Mitigation**: Adjusts execution based on current liquidity and price pressure
- **Dynamic Risk Adjustment**: Pauses or throttles order flow in response to volatility or network congestion

AI-based risk controls also provide:

- **Pre-trade risk assessment**: Simulates outcomes before placing large orders
- **Post-trade analytics**: Analyzes market impact and refines strategies

Checklist for SMB Traders:

- ☑ Integrate real-time market data feeds with your execution layer
- ☑ Use AI models trained on venue-specific characteristics
- ☑ Monitor latency and queue position effects continuously

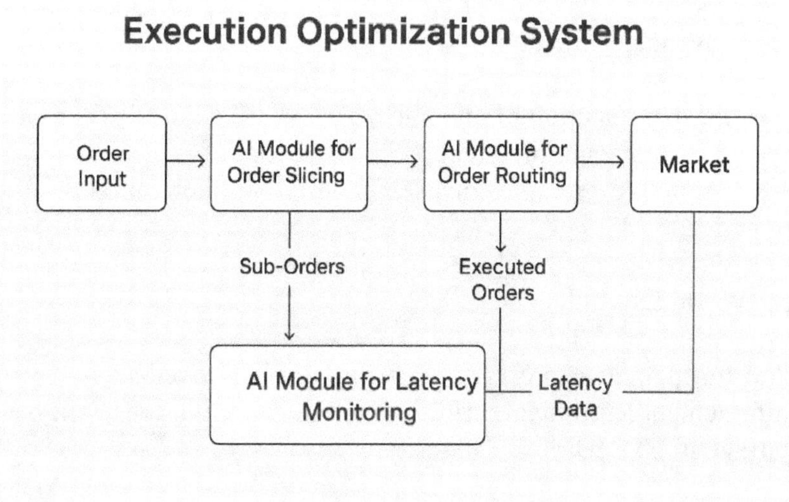

AI-Driven Arbitrage and Speed Advantages

Arbitrage opportunities are short-lived price discrepancies across markets. AI identifies and capitalizes on these differences faster than traditional systems.

Arbitrage Strategies Enhanced by AI:

- **Triangular Arbitrage**: Involves three currencies or assets in a loop
- **Statistical Arbitrage**: Detects deviations from historical price correlations
- **Cross-Exchange Arbitrage**: Exploits differences in asset prices across venues

Speed advantages include:

- Faster detection of anomalies
- Lower execution latency via co-location
- Adaptive strategies that self-modify based on market feedback

Real-World Example:

What happened: A proprietary trading firm deployed a reinforcement learning algorithm to optimize timing for latency arbitrage in ETF pairs.

What went right: Annualized returns increased 9% without increasing trade frequency.

What we learn: Speed alone isn't enough—adaptive timing matters.

[INSERT IMAGE: Arbitrage opportunity tracker visualization comparing asset prices across exchanges with AI decision overlay]

Regulatory Risks & Flash Crash Concerns

With speed and autonomy comes systemic risk. Flash crashes—sudden, deep price drops triggered by automated feedback loops—are an ever-present threat.

Key Incidents:

- **May 6, 2010 Flash Crash**: Dow plunged 1,000 points in minutes
- **2020 Oil Market Crash**: Algo trading exacerbated price collapse

Regulatory Focus:

- **SEC (U.S.)**: Requires algorithm documentation, kill switches, and pre-trade risk checks
- **ESMA (EU)**: Enforces MiFID II obligations on algo and HFT traders
- **ASIC (Australia)**: Mandates venue-specific compliance for HFT access

Risk Mitigation Tactics:

- ☑ Implement circuit breakers and throttling mechanisms
- ☑ Conduct backtesting in live market replay environments
- ☑ Maintain a kill switch with real-time override capabilities

Common Pitfalls:

- Over-optimization for historical data leading to fragility
- Lack of governance over model updates
- Ignoring inter-algo interaction effects (one bot triggers another)

Conclusion

AI has permanently changed the game in algorithmic and high-frequency trading. From microstructure pattern detection to execution optimization and adaptive arbitrage, intelligent systems now compete at a level—and speed—that human traders cannot match.

But high performance comes with high risk. Transparency, fail-safes, and continuous oversight are essential—not optional.

For SMBs, entering the AI-algo arena means investing not just in models, but in discipline: model governance, latency engineering, and regulatory foresight.

Next Steps

- Evaluate your current trading system's ability to support AI inputs
- Identify a specific use case (e.g., execution quality, slippage reduction) for pilot deployment
- Partner with vendors offering real-time data integration and model tuning
- Review your compliance framework for HFT and algo audit readiness
- Implement circuit breakers and scenario testing for system resilience

Next up: Chapter 10, *AI Ethics & Bias in Finance*, tackles the toughest questions in AI deployment—black box opacity, ethical constraints, fairness audits, and what responsible AI looks like in a regulated financial world.

Chapter 10: AI Ethics & Bias in Finance

Artificial intelligence is transforming finance—but not always transparently or fairly. As firms deploy increasingly powerful models to make decisions about credit, investment, and risk, they face a profound challenge: how to build systems that are not only effective, but also ethical.

Bias, opacity, and unaccountable automation can damage reputations, trigger regulatory fines, and exclude vulnerable customers. And while large institutions may have compliance teams and legal firewalls, SMBs often lack the guardrails to spot problems before they cause harm. This chapter examines the real risks of AI in finance—technical, ethical, and regulatory—and provides frameworks for deploying responsible, auditable systems.

The Black Box Problem in AI Finance

AI systems often operate as black boxes—delivering decisions or scores without clear explanations. This creates problems in finance where transparency, accountability, and compliance are non-negotiable.

Why It's a Problem:

- **Auditability**: Regulators may require documentation of how a loan was denied
- **Customer Trust**: Consumers demand to know why they're rejected or flagged
- **Internal Risk**: If a model malfunctions, can your team explain what went wrong?

Black-box models are particularly dangerous when they:

- Use ensemble techniques (e.g., random forests + neural nets)
- Lack feature importance outputs
- Rely on high-cardinality categorical variables (e.g., ZIP codes)

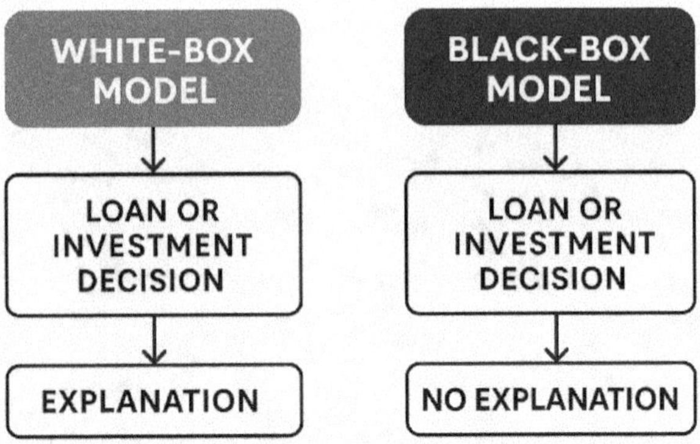

Checklist for Mitigation:

- ☑ Prioritize models with built-in explainability (e.g., decision trees, interpretable ML)
- ☑ Use post-hoc explainers like SHAP or LIME
- ☑ Log decision paths and model metadata for audits

Bias in Credit, Investment, and Risk Models

Bias in AI can take many forms—and financial AI is particularly vulnerable because it uses real-world historical data, which reflects real-world inequality.

Bias Sources:

- **Training Data**: Biased past approvals reinforce biased future predictions
- **Feature Selection**: Seemingly neutral features act as proxies (e.g., address = race)
- **Labeling Bias**: Default vs non-default labels are influenced by systemic access to capital

Where It Shows Up:

- **Credit Scoring**: Minority applicants rejected more often for equivalent profiles
- **Investment Recommendations**: Lower asset allocations for women or younger users
- **Insurance Risk Scores**: Penalize drivers in low-income neighborhoods

Real-World Case:

What happened: A large U.S. bank was investigated for offering higher interest rates to minority borrowers via an AI pricing engine.

What went wrong: The system had learned correlations from historic lending behavior, not actual risk.

What we learn: AI can replicate human bias at scale—and hide it in layers of math.

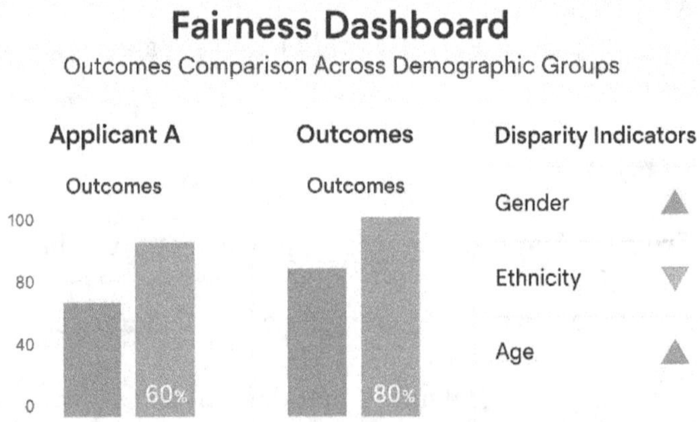

Explainability & Model Auditing Techniques

Explainability is not a nice-to-have—it's now a legal and ethical requirement in many jurisdictions. But just showing a prediction score isn't enough. Firms must explain:

- What data was used
- What features drove the decision
- What alternatives were considered

Leading Tools:

- **SHAP**: Shows how much each input contributed to a prediction
- **LIME**: Explains individual predictions by approximating them with interpretable models
- **Fairlearn & Aequitas**: Open-source toolkits for bias measurement and mitigation

Auditing Workflow:

1. Train model on representative data
2. Test on disaggregated groups
3. Run fairness metrics (equal opportunity, demographic parity)
4. Generate local and global explanations
5. Document findings and store for regulator or stakeholder review

Checklist for SMBs:

- ☑ Choose vendors that provide explainability APIs or dashboards
- ☑ Perform annual fairness and explainability audits
- ☑ Train teams to interpret model audit outputs and communicate them to stakeholders

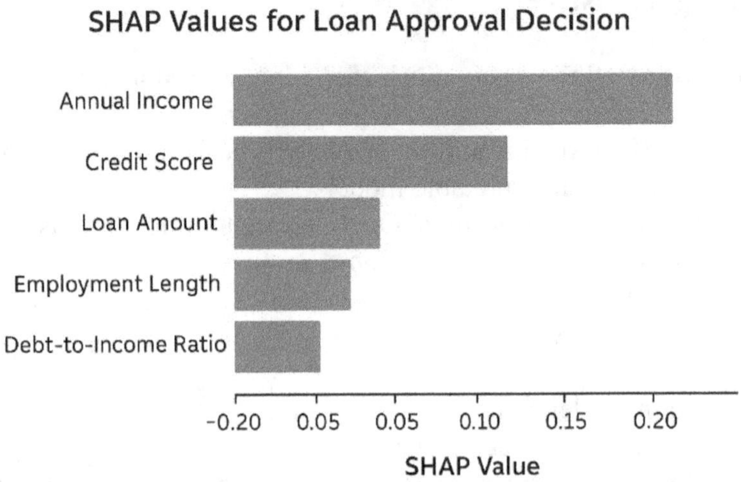

Principles of Ethical AI in FinTech

Ethical AI is not just about compliance—it's about building systems that earn trust, reduce harm, and align with your mission.

Core Principles:

- **Transparency**: Users and regulators can understand decisions
- **Accountability**: Humans are ultimately responsible for outcomes
- **Fairness**: Similar users get similar treatment
- **Autonomy**: Users can override or appeal automated decisions
- **Privacy**: Data is collected and used with consent and purpose

Real-World Example:

What happened: A fintech lender integrated an AI loan assistant that recommended higher repayment plans than needed, increasing default risk.

What went right: The firm introduced a second-model check and disclosed rationale to the user, who could request a review.

What we learn: Transparency builds resilience—and brand trust.

Tactical Implementation:

- ☑ Publish an internal AI ethics policy
- ☑ Form a cross-functional AI ethics review board
- ☑ Define model lifecycles with fairness and privacy checkpoints

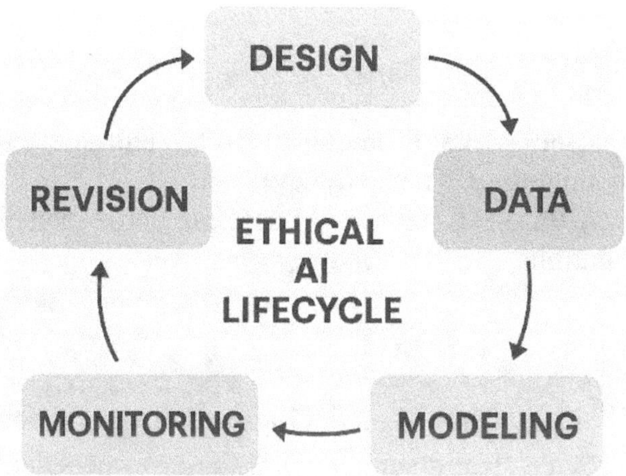

Regulatory and Compliance Frameworks

Around the world, regulators are stepping in to shape how AI is used in finance. Whether you operate locally or globally, your models must align with emerging frameworks.

U.S.:

- **CFPB**: Scrutinizing credit scoring AI for discrimination
- **FTC**: Investigating "unfair or deceptive" AI practices
- **SEC**: Mandates for model explainability in investment advisory

Europe:

- **EU AI Act**: Requires human oversight for high-risk AI systems like lending and insurance
- **GDPR**: Right to explanation for algorithmic decisions

Asia-Pacific:

- **Singapore MAS**: Promotes "FEAT" (Fairness, Ethics, Accountability, Transparency)
- **Australia ASIC**: Guides AI usage under responsible lending obligations

SMBs must:

- ☑ Maintain detailed model logs and change histories
- ☑ Provide clear documentation for customers denied service or flagged by AI
- ☑ Stay updated on national-level regulation rollouts

Conclusion

AI in finance is powerful—but power without principles is dangerous. Ethical, explainable, and fair AI isn't just a compliance goal—it's a business advantage.

Customers trust brands that treat them with transparency. Regulators favor firms that document and govern their models. And teams operate more confidently when they know how their tools work.

Finance's future will be built by those who get AI right—not just fast.

Next Steps

- Audit your current AI systems for explainability and bias risk
- Choose an explainability tool and integrate it into your review pipeline
- Document your AI models' decisions, fairness metrics, and oversight process
- Train staff across departments on ethical AI basics

Next: Chapter 11, *FinTech Startups & Innovation*, dives into how new ventures are reimagining finance using AI, from lending disruptors to data-first wealthtech platforms.

Chapter 11: FinTech Startups & Innovation

Innovation in finance no longer comes from legacy institutions—it comes from small, fast-moving, AI-first startups. Across lending, wealth management, payments, and insurance, startups are using artificial intelligence not just to optimize existing systems, but to reimagine what financial services can be.

In this chapter, we explore how FinTech startups are driving disruption, where they're finding the edge in data and AI strategy, and the challenges they face as they scale—from regulation to funding to infrastructure. For founders, investors, and SMB leaders, this chapter offers both a playbook and a competitive lens.

How Startups Are Reimagining Finance with AI

Startups aren't just deploying AI—they're building business models around it. Unlike legacy firms trying to retrofit AI onto outdated tech stacks, AI-native startups treat intelligence, automation, and prediction as core value propositions.

What AI Changes:

- **Speed**: Instant loan approvals, personalized portfolio updates, fraud alerts in seconds
- **Scale**: AI doesn't scale linearly—once trained, it serves millions
- **Cost**: AI automates tasks that used to require entire departments

Startups win by:

- Embedding AI into customer experience—not just backend ops
- Solving niche problems with narrow, deep intelligence
- Building data infrastructure from day one

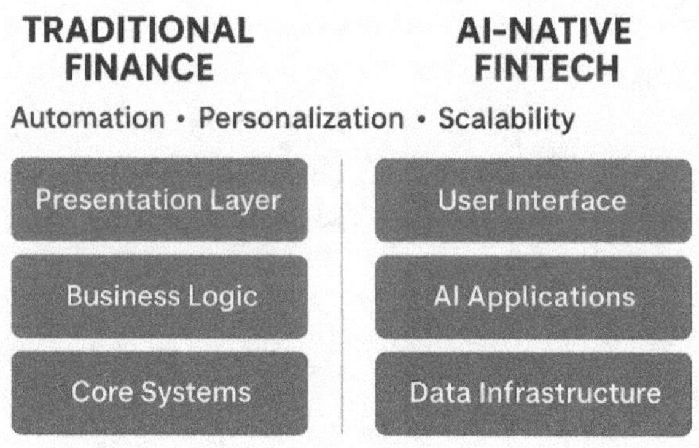

Real-World Startup: **Zest AI**

What they do: Replaces traditional credit underwriting with AI scoring

Why it matters: Enables lenders to serve more borrowers without increasing default risk

Key lesson: Startups succeed when they align AI capabilities with underserved financial needs

Disruptive AI Applications in Lending, WealthTech

The most mature FinTech categories for AI disruption are lending and wealth management.

Lending:

- **Automated Underwriting**: AI processes applications in minutes, not days
- **Alternative Credit Scoring**: Analyzes cash flow, rent, and phone data
- **Fraud Detection**: Flags synthetic identities and document tampering in real time

Example: **Upstart**

- Uses AI to price credit risk for non-prime borrowers
- Reports 27% lower loss rates at the same approval rate as traditional lenders

WealthTech:

- **Robo-Advisors**: Personalize asset allocation based on real-time behavior
- **Behavioral Nudges**: AI detects and corrects suboptimal investor moves
- **Predictive Planning**: Forecasts future savings needs based on lifestyle signals

Example: **Betterment**

- AI adjusts investment plans based on goals, income shifts, and market changes

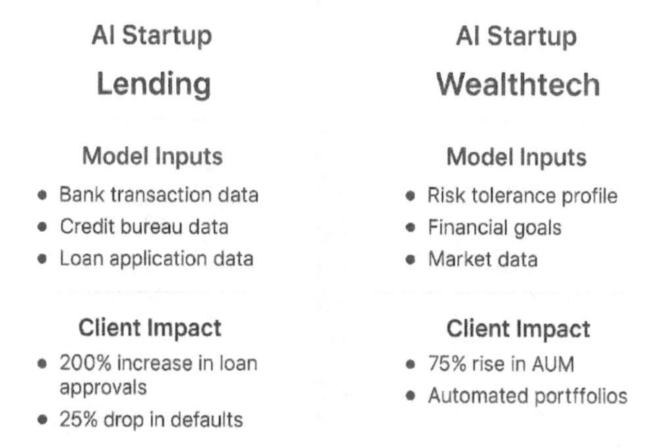

Data Differentiation in AI-First Startups

In AI-first companies, data is not a byproduct—it's the product. The most valuable startups are not those with the best models, but those with the best **data flywheels**.

What Differentiates Winners:

- **Proprietary Data Access**: Direct integration with user platforms or financial behavior
- **Real-Time Labeling**: Feedback loops from customer outcomes to model training
- **Data Network Effects**: More users = better models = better experience = more users

Startup Spotlight: **Plaid**

- Not an AI tool—but a data infrastructure layer for others to build intelligent systems
- Powers many lending and budgeting tools by enabling permissioned financial data sharing

Checklist for Founders:

- ☑ Build data pipelines before AI models
- ☑ Focus on quality and labeling, not just quantity
- ☑ Use anonymized cohort insights to comply with privacy and still generate value

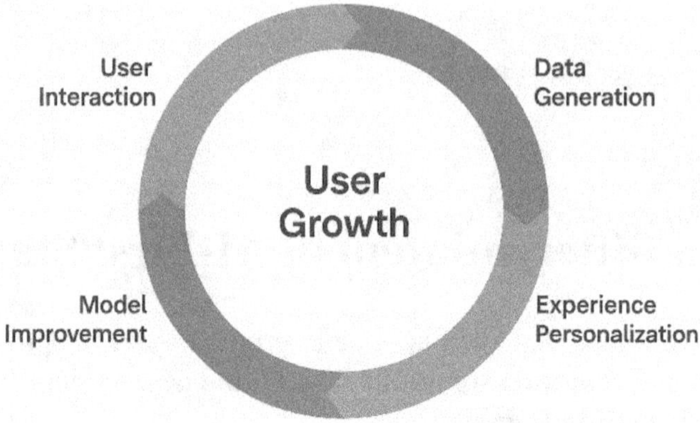

Scaling, Funding, and Regulatory Hurdles

AI-based FinTechs face a steep climb from MVP to market dominance. The biggest roadblocks aren't technical—they're financial and regulatory.

Scaling AI Startups:

- **Model Governance**: Each new product requires new explainability, fairness, and risk controls
- **Infrastructure**: Moving from notebooks to production-grade ML ops
- **Talent**: Finding engineers who understand both AI and compliance

Funding AI Startups:

Investors now demand:

- Demonstrated ROI from AI, not just potential
- Clear IP around data or models
- Path to defensible margins despite cloud costs

Regulatory Complexity:

- Early-stage startups often operate in gray zones (e.g., automated advice, lending)
- Compliance is often an afterthought—until growth attracts scrutiny
- Founders must engage with regulators early, not wait for Series C

Checklist for Startups:

- ☑ Hire a compliance advisor before product launch
- ☑ Build a sandbox for regulators to see models in action
- ☑ Document your model lifecycle from Day 1

Growts Stage	AI Milestones	Compliance Milestones	Infrastructure Milestones
Seed	MVP Model Development	Regulatory Assessment	Basic Cloud Setup
Series A	Initial Model Deployment	Data Governance Framework	Data Pipeline Development
Series B	Model Scaling & Optimization	Risk & Audit Controls	High Availability Systems
Series C	Advanced Model Capabilities	Full Regulatory Compliance	Robust IT Infrastructure

Top Emerging FinTech AI Innovators to Watch

These startups exemplify innovation, traction, and responsibility:

- **Tala**: Mobile-first microloans using smartphone data (Africa, Asia, Latin America)
- **Petal**: Credit cards using cash flow underwriting instead of credit scores
- **Albert**: AI-powered financial assistant that helps users save and budget
- **TruEra**: Model explainability and monitoring platform for responsible AI
- **Symend**: Behaviorally intelligent debt collection using NLP and predictive models

What They Have in Common:

- AI models trained on non-traditional signals
- Consumer-centric design
- Built-in explainability and fairness monitoring

Conclusion

The FinTech revolution is being led by startups that treat AI not as an add-on, but as a business model foundation. They're solving real problems—faster underwriting, inclusive finance, better planning—using smarter data and leaner operations.

But speed without trust won't scale. The next generation of AI FinTechs must master not just intelligence, but accountability.

Next Steps

- Identify an area in your own firm or market where AI-native FinTechs are gaining share
- Evaluate whether your tech stack can support AI-powered features or partnerships
- Build or license your data infrastructure before launching AI products
- Prioritize explainability, compliance, and user control from MVP to maturity

Next: Chapter 12, *AI in AML and Regulatory Compliance*, explores how AI is transforming anti-money laundering, identity verification, and compliance workflows worldwide.

Chapter 12: AI in AML and Regulatory Compliance

Anti-money laundering (AML) and regulatory compliance are two of the most operationally burdensome areas in finance—especially for institutions trying to scale across borders or product lines. The cost of compliance is high, and the cost of non-compliance is even higher.

Artificial intelligence offers a way forward—not just through automation, but through intelligence. Modern AI systems can scan millions of transactions, detect suspicious behavior, flag false positives with greater accuracy, and even verify identities through biometric and document analysis. This chapter outlines how AI is revolutionizing AML and regulatory functions, and how SMBs and FinTechs can deploy these tools responsibly.

Automating AML/KYC with AI

Know Your Customer (KYC) and AML procedures are essential—but often repetitive and slow. AI transforms these workflows by:

- **Automating Document Checks**: OCR + NLP to validate IDs, utility bills, and financial statements
- **Risk Scoring**: Machine learning models assign risk scores based on activity and profile
- **Workflow Routing**: AI prioritizes high-risk cases for human review, reducing analyst load

Example: **Trulioo** and **Onfido** provide AI-powered KYC tools used by banks, payment platforms, and crypto firms.

Benefits:

- Cuts onboarding time from days to minutes
- Reduces manual labor costs
- Enhances fraud detection with behavioral overlays

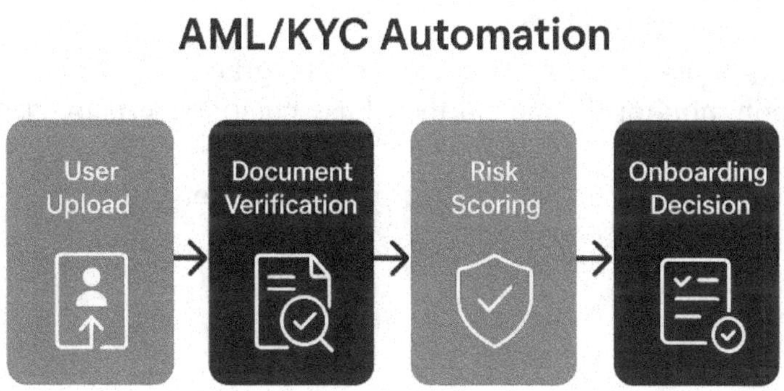

Checklist:

- ☑ Use supervised models trained on real fraud patterns
- ☑ Combine AI with human review for high-value customers
- ☑ Maintain audit trails of decisions for compliance readiness

AI for Transaction Monitoring & Alerts

Traditional transaction monitoring systems produce thousands of alerts daily—most of which are false positives. AI improves accuracy and context.

Key Capabilities:

- **Behavioral Baselines**: AI models learn normal user behavior and flag anomalies
- **Real-Time Risk Scoring**: Each transaction is scored dynamically
- **Unsupervised Learning**: Detects novel fraud or laundering schemes not seen in training data

Real-World Use Case:

What happened: A European neobank integrated AI-driven transaction monitoring and cut their false positive alerts by 70%.

What we learn: AI doesn't just improve detection—it reduces noise and speeds resolution.

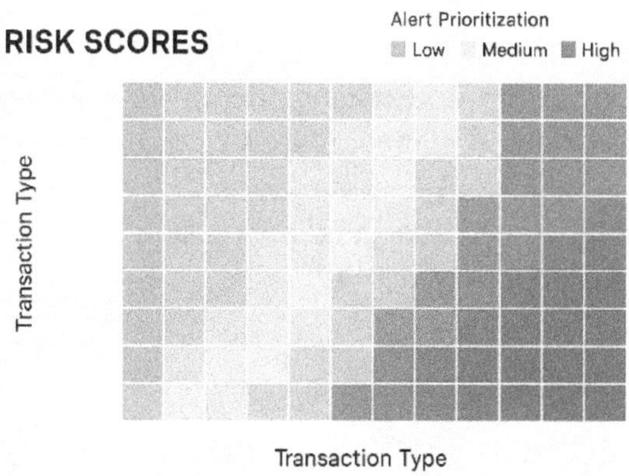

Tactical Tips:

- ☑ Retrain models monthly to adapt to new fraud vectors
- ☑ Cross-reference transactions with global watchlists
- ☑ Log explanations for each alert trigger

Identity Verification with Computer Vision

Computer vision, paired with AI, allows firms to verify identity documents, match selfies to IDs, and detect forgeries.

Applications:

- **Facial Recognition**: Confirms liveness and prevents impersonation
- **Document Authenticity**: Detects tampering in passports, licenses, and more
- **Geo-Validation**: Ensures document origin matches user geography

Vendors like Jumio and Veriff combine deep learning with image forensics to offer compliant, scalable verification.

Use Case:

What happened: A crypto exchange deployed CV-based onboarding and dropped manual review rates by 60%.

What went right: Speed and fraud prevention both improved, while KYC cost per user decreased.

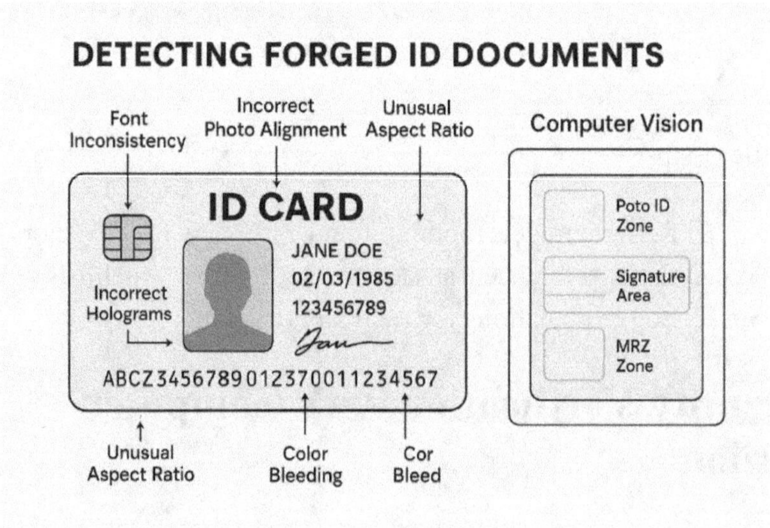

SMB Implementation Tips:

- ☑ Use passive liveness detection to avoid user friction
- ☑ Regularly evaluate model accuracy on diverse demographics
- ☑ Ensure GDPR/CCPA compliance for biometric data storage

Reducing False Positives in Compliance

False positives are one of the biggest inefficiencies in AML. Every unnecessary alert costs time, delays onboarding, and frustrates users.

AI reduces false positives by:

- **Contextualizing Activity**: Considers customer profile and intent
- **Reinforcement Learning**: Learns from prior case outcomes to improve precision
- **Entity Resolution**: Matches aliases and variations to avoid duplicate reviews

Example: A U.S. brokerage reduced case investigation time by 45% using AI clustering and auto-dismissal tools.

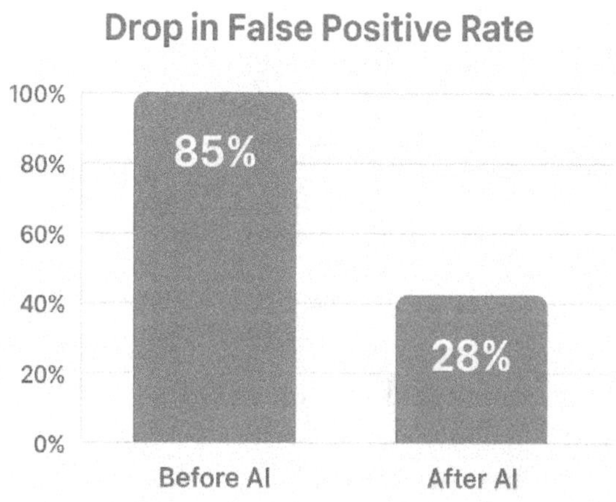

Checklist:

- ☑ Track false positive rate as a key compliance KPI
- ☑ Allow human feedback to retrain model thresholds
- ☑ Integrate AI alerts into case management systems

Regulatory Tech and Global Frameworks

Compliance is no longer a manual process—it's a technology race. RegTech platforms now integrate AI for proactive, auditable compliance.

Key Regulatory Frameworks Influencing AI Use:

- **FATF**: Global AML guidelines emphasizing "risk-based approach"
- **EU AMLA**: Requires enhanced due diligence and monitoring via tech
- **BSA/AML (U.S.)**: Encourages innovation in AI for AML monitoring

Leading RegTech Capabilities:

- Dynamic rule tuning
- Real-time risk dashboards
- Integrated watchlist scanning (OFAC, PEP, Interpol)
- Audit trail generation and version control

Vendor Spotlight: **ComplyAdvantage**

- AI-driven adverse media and sanction screening
- Used by mid-market and enterprise clients for scalable global compliance

Conclusion

AML and compliance are no longer just about defense—they're about competitive advantage. AI enables faster onboarding, smarter monitoring, and lower operating costs while staying ahead of global regulatory complexity.

For SMBs, smart compliance isn't optional—it's how you stay in business and scale responsibly.

Next Steps

- Audit your current AML/KYC pipeline for manual bottlenecks
- Choose one AI-enhanced tool to pilot (e.g., transaction risk scoring or document verification)
- Track false positive rate, onboarding time, and regulatory audit outcomes
- Ensure all AI tools include explainability, audit logging, and data retention controls

Next: Chapter 13, *AI-Powered Customer Experience*, explores how AI is transforming service, support, and personalization for financial clients across every channel.

Chapter 13: AI-Powered Customer Experience

Customer expectations in finance have changed. Speed, personalization, and 24/7 availability are no longer luxuries—they're table stakes. AI is now the engine powering this transformation. It's not just behind the scenes; it's right in front of the user, embedded in every touchpoint: the chatbot answering mortgage questions, the voice assistant checking account balances, the predictive model suggesting a better credit card.

In this chapter, we explore how AI is reshaping the customer experience across banking, investment, and financial support services—and what SMBs need to know to build trust, drive engagement, and deliver intelligent service at scale.

AI Chatbots in Banking & Wealth Services

AI chatbots have rapidly evolved from scripted helpers to dynamic, context-aware financial assistants. They can:

- Handle balance inquiries, transaction lookups, and account updates
- Answer product and policy questions
- Onboard new customers with guided flows
- Help users find the right savings, loan, or investment option

How They Work:

- NLP engines interpret user input
- Intent recognition routes the request
- Integrated APIs pull real-time data
- Machine learning continuously refines responses

Example: **Erica** (Bank of America) has handled over a billion interactions, from alerts to spending insights.

Checklist for Effective Chatbot Deployment:

- ☑ Train on real financial queries, not generic phrases
- ☑ Include escalation to human agents when confidence is low
- ☑ Log queries to improve both FAQ and model performance

Conversational AI & Voice Recognition

Conversational AI extends chatbots into spoken interactions. With smart speakers and mobile voice assistants, financial firms can:

- Enable hands-free banking
- Provide real-time budget updates
- Allow users to pay bills or transfer funds using voice commands

Core Technologies:

- **ASR (Automatic Speech Recognition)**
- **NLU (Natural Language Understanding)**
- **TTS (Text-to-Speech)**

Example: **Capital One's Alexa skill** allows users to check balances, track spending, and pay credit cards via voice.

Security Considerations:

- Use biometric verification (voiceprint or device-based)
- Require multi-factor confirmation for sensitive tasks
- Detect and block spoofed or replayed voice commands

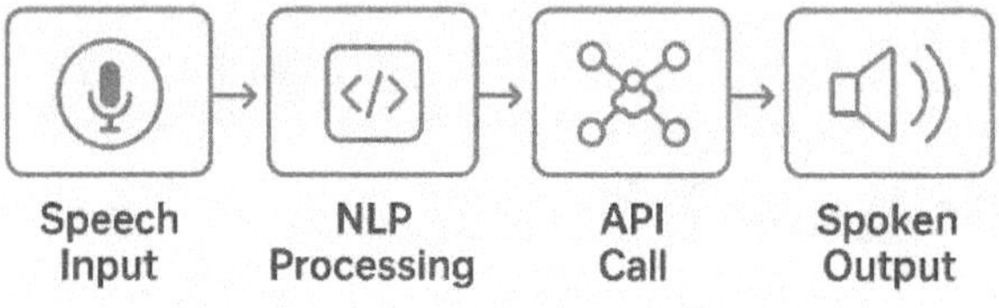

Personalized Financial Product Offers

AI systems can analyze user behavior, transaction history, and life stage indicators to recommend highly relevant products—at just the right time.

What AI Personalization Looks At:

- Spending patterns (travel, dining, recurring subscriptions)
- Life events (income changes, new dependents, address changes)
- Risk profile and financial goals.

Use Cases:

- Suggesting a lower-fee investment product
- Offering pre-approved credit with optimized terms
- Nudging users toward savings boosters during income spikes

Example: **Chime** uses AI to personalize messaging and product nudges based on user financial habits and goals.

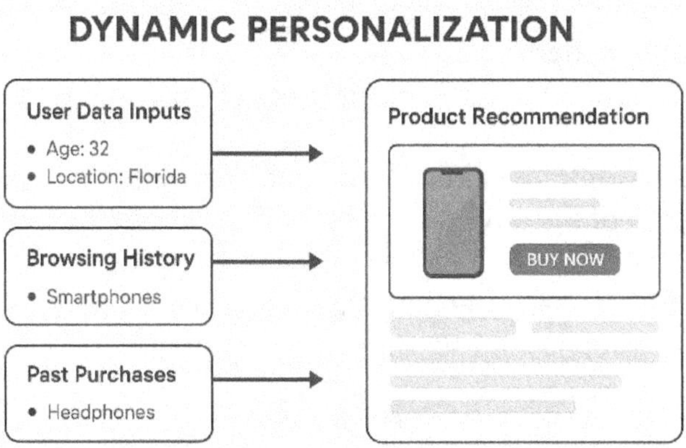

Common Pitfalls:

- Over-targeting or appearing too invasive
- Recommending irrelevant or high-risk products
- Ignoring user feedback loops

Checklist:

- ☑ Start with opt-in personalization
- ☑ Allow product offer suppression or tuning
- ☑ Use explainable AI to clarify why an offer is being shown

AI for Fraud Alerts & 24/7 Support

Customers want to feel safe—and informed. AI enables real-time fraud detection and always-on support without overloading service teams.

Key Features:

- **Anomaly Detection**: Flags suspicious login or spending activity instantly
- **Behavioral Biometrics**: Recognizes typical device, location, typing patterns
- **Proactive Alerts**: Notifies users of potential fraud or account issues
- **AI Support Agents**: Resolve low-complexity tickets and route complex ones

Example: **HSBC** uses machine learning to detect card fraud and reduce false declines, preserving customer trust.

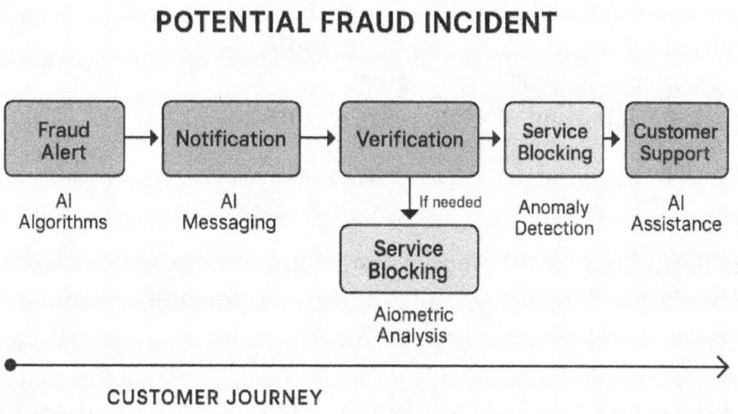

Checklist for Support AI:

- ☑ Integrate with CRM for context-aware responses
- ☑ Build fallback flows for technical or emotional complexity
- ☑ Measure resolution time, satisfaction, and false positive rates

Trust & Adoption of Customer-Facing AI

Even the smartest AI won't succeed without customer trust. Transparency, control, and performance are essential.

How to Build Trust:

- **Explainability**: Show users why they received an offer or decision
- **Consistency**: Responses must match brand tone and policy
- **Control**: Users should opt in to AI services, with clear settings and overrides

Barriers to Adoption:

- Fear of automation replacing human touch
- Unclear data usage policies
- Poor handling of edge cases or errors

Real-World Example:

What happened: A robo-advisor startup offered fully automated planning but added an "Ask an Advisor" button after customer pushback.

What went right: Trust and adoption both increased as users saw AI as support, not replacement.

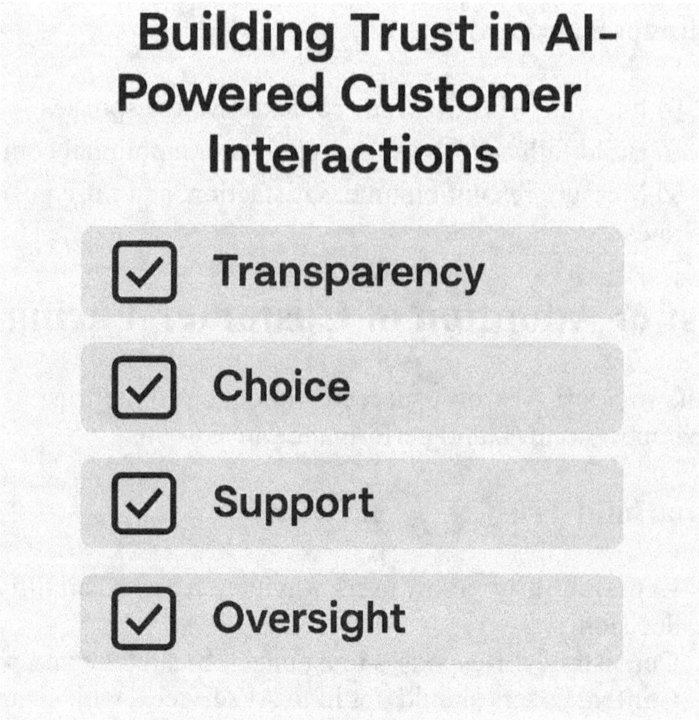

Conclusion

AI is no longer a back-office tool—it's at the heart of the customer experience. From chatbots and voice assistants to proactive fraud alerts and personalized offers, AI is now the interface between financial firms and the people they serve.

But AI only adds value when it adds clarity, relevance, and reliability. The best customer experiences combine AI's intelligence with human empathy and transparency.

For SMBs and fintechs, the opportunity is clear: AI-driven service isn't just about doing more—it's about doing it better, faster, and more personally.

Next Steps

- Audit your customer interaction channels for AI readiness (chat, voice, mobile)
- Identify a use case to pilot—fraud alerts, savings nudges, or onboarding chat
- Choose platforms that support explainability and human fallback
- Train staff on how to work alongside AI, not compete with it

Next: Chapter 14, *Future Trends: Quantum AI & Autonomous Finance*, takes a forward-looking view at what's coming next—from self-managing money to edge AI to the implications of quantum computing in finance.

Chapter 14: Future Trends: Quantum AI & Autonomous Finance

Most chapters in this book have focused on what's here now—tools that today's SMBs and FinTech teams can evaluate, implement, and use to reduce cost or unlock opportunity. But as AI continues its acceleration, the financial systems of the future will begin to look fundamentally different. Quantum computing, agent-based automation, and edge deployment will play defining roles.

This chapter explores the bleeding edge of what's possible and probable. These trends may not be deployable tomorrow—but they shape the roadmap for the next decade and beyond. Financial leaders who prepare for these trajectories early will be best positioned to lead in 2035 and beyond.

What Is Quantum AI & Why It's Relevant

Quantum AI refers to the intersection of quantum computing and artificial intelligence—two fields that, together, could supercharge processing power and enable entirely new types of models.

Why It Matters to Finance:

- **Speed**: Quantum processors could reduce training times from weeks to minutes for complex models
- **Combinatorics**: Finance often deals with portfolio optimization, derivatives pricing, and risk analysis—all problems with massive variable sets
- **New Model Architectures**: Quantum-native algorithms could outperform classical AI in multi-dimensional forecasting and financial simulation

Real-World Signals:

- IBM and Google are both investing in quantum-classical hybrid systems
- Goldman Sachs is exploring quantum use cases for pricing and arbitrage
- Quantum ML frameworks like PennyLane and Qiskit are emerging in developer communities

Quantum AI isn't ready for widespread deployment—but finance is a high-value early target. SMBs won't be running quantum backends, but they may license or benefit from cloud-hosted quantum APIs within a decade.

Self-Managing Money & AI Agents

One of the most disruptive ideas in finance is the notion of money that manages itself. AI agents could eventually:

- Move funds between accounts based on yield and risk tolerance
- Adjust insurance coverage automatically as life circumstances change
- Switch between investments in real-time to maintain risk-adjusted return

Key Capabilities:

- **Autonomous Action**: Agents execute without needing human input every time
- **Goal-Based Logic**: Agents are configured to optimize for specific outcomes (e.g., max savings, min risk)
- **Multi-Modal Learning**: Agents consider market data, user behavior, and regulatory rules

Use Case:

What happened: A next-gen robo-platform began testing "sweep intelligence" that reallocated idle checking balances nightly based on short-term yield curves.

What went right: Users passively earned more, with no extra clicks. Engagement and retention improved.

What we learn: When financial AI moves from advising to acting, the definition of service changes.

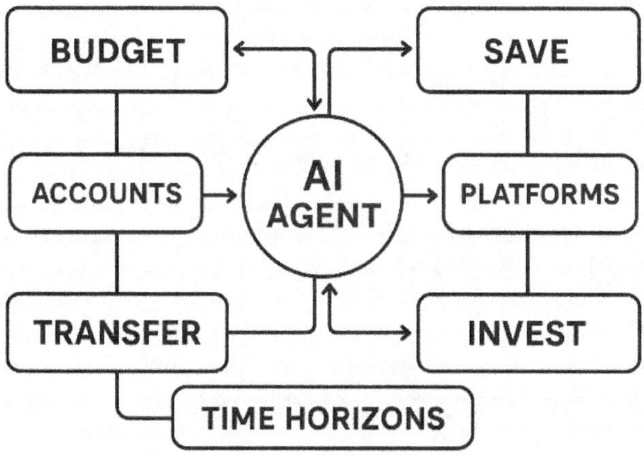

Autonomous Wealth Management Systems

Beyond single-agent functions, the next phase is full autonomy across an entire financial relationship. Imagine:

- An AI advisor that optimizes across investments, debt, insurance, and taxes
- An autonomous wealth entity acting in the background with user-defined parameters
- A world where people no longer "manage money" but set goals and let systems execute

Core Components:

- **Unified Data Layer**: Full financial visibility (banking, brokerage, real assets)
- **Action Engines**: Modular APIs for rebalancing, purchasing, switching providers
- **Personal Risk and Life Models**: Customized to the user and dynamically updated

Challenges:

- Legal clarity on agent authority and reversibility
- Building trust in actions taken without user review
- Integrating fragmented financial APIs across providers

This isn't science fiction—it's being piloted in wealth platforms, family office tech, and high-net-worth solutions. Democratization will follow.

Edge AI in Finance Devices

While most financial AI today lives in the cloud, the future includes smart agents on the edge—in smartphones, wearables, even payment hardware.

Examples:

- **Smart Cards**: Dynamic spending limits and real-time fraud detection built into the chip
- **Wearable Budgeting**: Alerts on wrist or phone based on spending triggers or voice input
- **ATM AI**: Personalized UX, facial recognition, and predictive cash withdrawal settings

Benefits of Edge AI:

- **Latency**: Real-time decisions without cloud dependency
- **Privacy**: Keeps personal data on device
- **Resilience**: Operates during network outages or disconnected environments

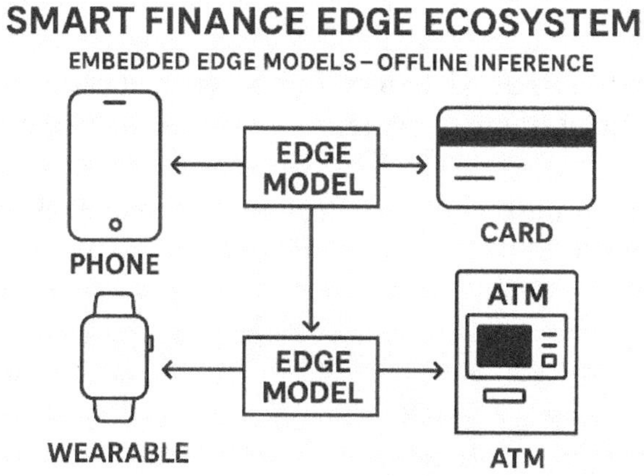

Implications for SMBs:

- App design must consider on-device ML and processing constraints
- Data synchronization becomes critical
- Customer experience will shift toward ambient, contextual interaction

Ethical and Speculative Forecasts (2035+)

With great power comes great risk. As financial AI gains autonomy, speed, and ubiquity, we must anticipate the ethical, legal, and societal implications.

Open Questions:

- Who's liable if an AI agent makes a costly decision?
- Will wealth gaps widen if the best autonomous tools are paywalled?
- How will regulators audit systems that learn and evolve in real time?

Speculative Trends:

- **Decentralized AI banks** with no human staff
- **Financial identity clones**—AI agents that negotiate on your behalf
- **Programmable privacy wallets** that choose when and what data to share

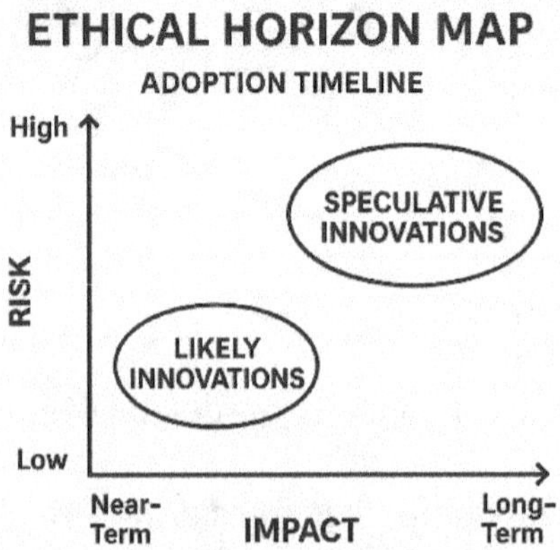

Call to Action:

- Start building explainability and override logic into every AI module
- Create governance frameworks for autonomy before it arrives
- Educate users and regulators—not just engineers

Conclusion

The future of finance is not just faster or smarter—it's increasingly autonomous. Quantum computing will expand what's computationally possible. AI agents will take over tasks we now think of as deeply personal. Edge AI will bring intelligence to the physical layer of transactions.

SMBs must not just watch these trends—they must prepare. The firms that win in 2035 will be those who start adapting now: experimenting with agents, investing in transparent automation, and architecting infrastructure for decentralized, intelligent systems.

Next Steps

- Map out which tasks in your finance org could become autonomous with clear parameters
- Monitor emerging vendor ecosystems in quantum simulation and AI agent orchestration
- Audit your current AI stack for future readiness: override logic, audit trails, and modular design
- Engage with your legal team on future-facing compliance scenarios

Next: Chapter 15, *Building an AI-First Finance Strategy*, shows how to convert insights from this book into a strategic roadmap—aligning leadership, teams, and tech to compete in the next era of finance.

Chapter 15: Building an AI-First Finance Strategy

Throughout this book, we've examined how artificial intelligence is changing finance—from fraud detection and credit scoring to wealth management and regulatory compliance. But none of that matters unless you can operationalize it. The final chapter is where insight becomes execution.

This is your roadmap for becoming an AI-first finance organization. Not an organization that simply adopts a few tools—but one that treats intelligence, automation, and learning as core capabilities. This chapter covers how to assess your readiness, structure a rollout plan, choose partners, measure success, and manage change across people, culture, and systems.

Assessing Your AI Readiness

Before diving into solutions, you need to evaluate your foundation. AI success isn't just about tech—it's about data, mindset, leadership, and architecture.

Key Readiness Factors:

- **Data Infrastructure**: Do you have structured, accessible, high-quality data?
- **Talent & Ownership**: Who will own AI deployment—IT, product, compliance?
- **Use Case Clarity**: Are your goals well-defined, measurable, and financially justifiable?
- **Executive Alignment**: Does your leadership team understand what AI can and can't do?

AI Maturity Levels:

1. **Exploring**: Ad hoc pilots, no formal governance
2. **Emerging**: Defined AI strategy, early deployment teams
3. **Operational**: Integrated AI in workflows, repeatable processes
4. **AI-First**: AI embedded in products, decisions, and planning

Checklist:

- ☑ Inventory current tools and data pipelines
- ☑ Run workshops with business and tech leads to identify AI bottlenecks or opportunities
- ☑ Use a readiness survey to benchmark team understanding and support

Building a Finance AI Roadmap (Tools, Teams, Timing)

An AI roadmap is not a Gantt chart. It's a living document that ties use cases to real outcomes and timelines to resource realities.

Roadmap Essentials:

- **Short-Term (3–6 months)**: Low-risk, high-value pilots (e.g., fraud alert scoring, chatbot trials)
- **Mid-Term (6–18 months)**: Integration into core processes (e.g., underwriting, personalization)
- **Long-Term (18–36 months)**: Foundational redesigns (e.g., autonomous financial agents)

Key Roles:

- **AI Product Owner**: Drives vision, metrics, and roadmap
- **Data Engineering Lead**: Ensures scalable, governed data flow
- **Compliance Partner**: Flags regulatory boundaries and audit needs
- **Executive Sponsor**: Keeps momentum and clears cross-functional roadblocks

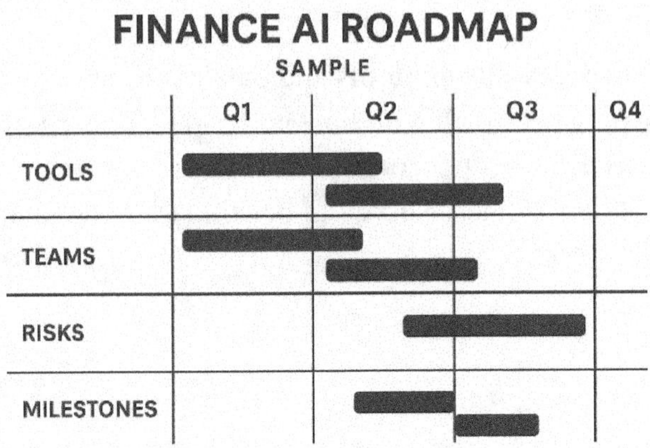

Pro Tips:

- Start with one function or customer journey
- Build for explainability and scale from Day 1
- Don't over-engineer—proof > perfection

In-House AI vs Vendor Partnerships

Should you build your own models—or buy from vendors? The answer is usually hybrid. It depends on your use case, data access, and team maturity.

When to Build:

- You have proprietary data that differentiates
- You need model transparency for compliance
- The use case is central to your core IP

When to Buy:

- You're solving common problems (e.g., KYC, chat, credit scoring)
- You lack model ops infrastructure
- Speed to value matters more than customization

Vendor Vetting Checklist:

- ☑ Can they explain their model architecture and logic?
- ☑ Do they offer APIs and deployment support?
- ☑ Are their data use terms, retention, and privacy policies clear?
- ☑ Do they support your regulatory and geographic needs?

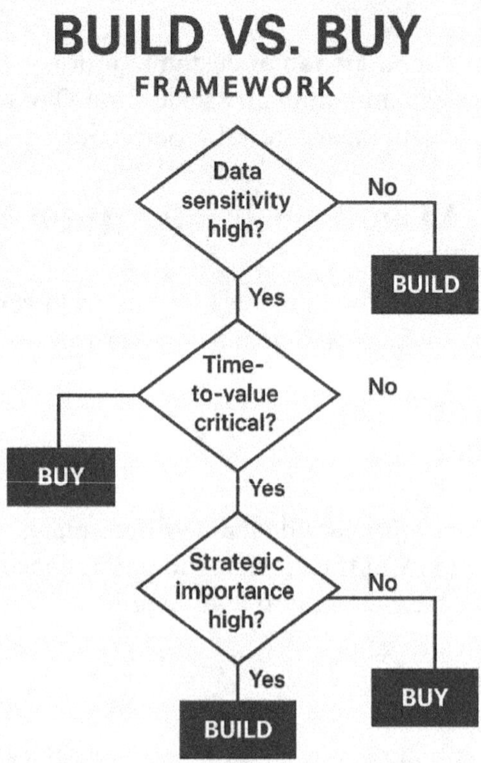

Key Success Metrics for AI Projects

AI success isn't just uptime—it's impact. Metrics must reflect both technical performance and business value.

Technical Metrics:

- Accuracy, precision, recall (for classification tasks)
- Drift detection and retraining frequency
- Latency and throughput (especially for real-time systems)

Business Metrics:

- Uplift vs baseline: How much more revenue, engagement, or efficiency?
- Customer impact: Are people getting better service, faster decisions?
- Compliance alignment: Are audits passing? Are regulators satisfied?

Use Case Example:

Use Case: AI-based transaction monitoring

- Precision: ↑ 55%
- Alert resolution time: ↓ 60%
- False positives: ↓ 40%

KPI DASHBOARD

FRAMEWORK

Technical Metrics

	AI Pilot 1	AI Pilot 2
Model Accuracy	85%	78%
Inference	120 min	135 min

Business Metrics

ROI	1500%	130%
Revenue Impact	$500K	$400K
	$200K	$150K
Cost Savings	$200K	$180K

Checklist:

- ☑ Define baseline performance before AI rollout
- ☑ Set target thresholds for business and tech metrics
- ☑ Use dashboards that unify model telemetry with business KPIs

Change Management & Executive Alignment

AI isn't just a tool—it's a cultural shift. It changes how decisions get made, how teams collaborate, and how customers are served.

Common Pitfalls:

- **Shadow Pilots**: Rogue experiments with no stakeholder visibility
- **Fear of Replacement**: Resistance from teams that see AI as a threat
- **Overhype or Under-delivery**: Unrealistic promises erode support

Change Drivers:

- **Transparent Communication**: Explain the why and how, not just the what
- **Collaborative Planning**: Co-create the roadmap with affected teams
- **Training & Reskilling**: Build AI fluency across roles—not just engineers

Executive Engagement:

- Frame AI as a competitive, not technical, advantage
- Tie success to revenue, retention, and risk reduction
- Create quarterly briefings with wins, learnings, and next moves

Conclusion

Becoming an AI-first finance organization isn't about having the most models or the biggest budget. It's about having clarity of purpose, consistency of execution, and the courage to lead with intelligence.

The SMBs and FinTechs that thrive over the next decade will be those who treat AI not as a project—but as a mindset. One rooted in transparency, measured impact, and relentless iteration.

The tools are here. The playbooks are clear. What's needed now is committed leadership and strategic discipline.

Final Action Plan

- Complete a team-wide AI readiness assessment
- Define 3–5 finance AI use cases tied to clear business outcomes
- Build a 12–24 month AI roadmap with owners and metrics
- Select one pilot to launch within 90 days
- Establish monthly governance checkpoints to review ethics, performance, and alignment

Thank you for reading. Your journey to AI-first finance doesn't end here—it begins here.

CHECK YOUR BONUS AT THE END !

Glossary of Terms

AI-First Organization – A company that embeds artificial intelligence into the core of its strategy, operations, and customer experience, treating AI as a foundational capability rather than a supplementary tool.

Artificial Intelligence (AI) – A branch of computer science that enables machines to simulate human intelligence through learning, reasoning, and self-correction.

Application Programming Interface (API) – A set of rules that allow different software systems to communicate and exchange data.

Automatic Speech Recognition (ASR) – Technology that converts spoken language into text, used in voice interfaces.

Behavioral Biometrics – The analysis of user behavior patterns such as typing speed, mouse movement, or swiping, used to verify identity or detect fraud.

Chatbot – An AI-powered interface that simulates human conversation to assist users with common inquiries or tasks.

Computer Vision (CV) – A field of AI that trains computers to interpret and process visual information from the world.

Data Flywheel – A self-reinforcing loop where user engagement generates more data, which improves models, which in turn enhance the product and attract more users.

Data Infrastructure – The systems and tools used to collect, store, manage, and process data.

Deep Learning – A subset of machine learning that uses neural networks with many layers to analyze complex patterns in large datasets.

Drift Detection – The monitoring of AI models for changes in input data or behavior that could degrade performance over time.

Edge AI – AI computations performed locally on devices (like phones or wearables), rather than in the cloud.

Explainable AI (XAI) – Tools and methods that make the predictions and logic of AI models understandable to humans.

False Positive – In AI detection, an instance where the model incorrectly flags something as a risk or match when it is not.

Fairness Audit – An assessment process that evaluates AI models for biased outcomes across demographic or protected groups.

High-Frequency Trading (HFT) – The use of algorithms to execute a large number of orders at extremely high speeds.

Know Your Customer (KYC) – A regulatory requirement where financial institutions verify the identity and risk level of their customers.

Machine Learning (ML) – A type of AI that enables systems to learn from data and improve performance without explicit programming.

Natural Language Processing (NLP) – A branch of AI that enables computers to understand, interpret, and generate human language.

Neural Network – A model architecture inspired by the human brain, often used in deep learning to recognize patterns in data.

Quantum AI – The integration of quantum computing with AI to solve complex problems faster than classical computing allows.

RegTech (Regulatory Technology) – The use of technology, including AI, to help businesses comply with regulations efficiently.

Reinforcement Learning – A machine learning technique where agents learn to make decisions through trial and error to maximize outcomes.

Risk Scoring – The use of models to assign a numerical score to the likelihood that a person or transaction represents a financial or compliance risk.

Robo-Advisor – A digital platform that provides automated, algorithm-driven financial planning services with minimal human supervision.

SHAP / LIME – Popular tools for interpreting complex machine learning models by showing feature contribution to predictions.

Synthetic Identity – A form of fraud where real and fake information are combined to create a new, false identity.

Text-to-Speech (TTS) – Converts written text into spoken voice output, often used in voice assistants.

Transaction Monitoring – The process of reviewing financial transactions to detect suspicious or illegal activity, often using AI.

Voiceprint – A unique vocal signature used in biometric authentication.

Watchlist Screening – The process of checking individuals or entities against global sanction or politically exposed person (PEP) lists.

Zero Trust – A security concept where no user or system is trusted by default, even if already inside the network perimeter.

This glossary is intended to support your continued learning and strategic application of AI in financial services. Use it as a reference throughout your implementation journey.

Bonus – FREE eBook Version

Want the full-color PDF version of this book?
Simply email me at **ericl@acrasolution.com** with a **screenshot of your Amazon purchase**, and I'll gladly send you your personal copy.

Thank you for taking the time to read this eBook.

Your support means more than you know. By purchasing and engaging with this book, you're directly contributing to the creation of more high-quality, practical resources for business owners, IT leaders, and professionals navigating the evolving landscape of financial technology and cybersecurity.

If you found value in this book, I'd be deeply grateful if you took a few minutes of your time to share your feedback. A positive review, a personal recommendation to a colleague, or simply applying what you've learned in your work all go a long way. Your encouragement helps fuel future writing, research, and tool development — and inspires continued work that makes a real difference in the business community.

If you'd like additional support or want to explore how we can help your organization implement what you've read, feel free to reach out or visit us online at www.acrasolution.com.

Thank you again for reading. Together, we can build a smarter, more secure financial future.

– Eric LeBouthillier
Founder, AcraSolution

www.ingramcontent.com/pod-product-compliance
Lightning Source LLC
LaVergne TN
LVHW022056200926
848481LV00003B/943
9781069643742